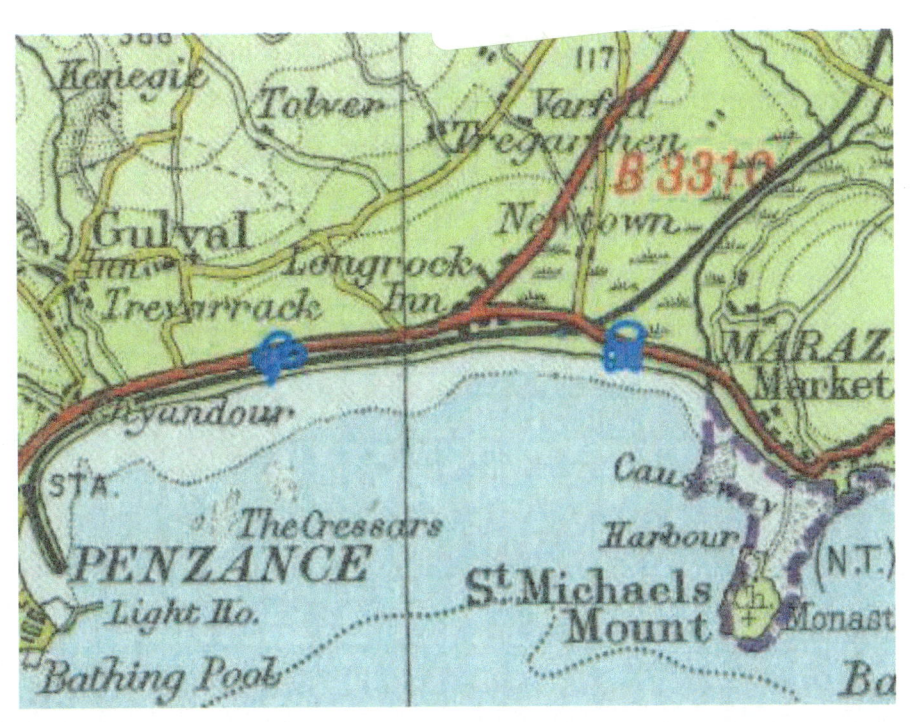

Above; The blue dots are more or less where we meet at Longrock Carpark on the left ending at Jordan's Cafe on the right. April 2025

Dear Nicky
Ray was my teacher during my recovery and I lost him suddenly in a similar way you lost your beloved Darren. You helped me through the grief like you have helped so many and I am so glad you remained on this Earth to do what you are doing. I am truly grateful. Call me if you want to do a foraging walk or stay in Cornwall.
Much love to you
Emma x

Disclaimer;

The aim of this book and walk is to inspire you to make coastal and hedgerow plants part of your everyday life. Its endeavour is to improve your physical and mental well being and understand how great nature is.

As the author I want to tell you I am not qualified in an official way either as a Doctor, herbalist or healer and therefore cannot directly recommend you to taste or use a plant in order to improve a disease or a limiting health condition. So if you do consume wild plants it will be at your own risk and it is always recommended to taste small amounts.

As well as the knowledge that Raymond taught me I will also be referring you to studies and books that present evidence or past teachings that would indicate beneficial uses of the plant. It is up to you to research and investigate these resources to make the best decision for you and your health and take precautions wherever necessary. Remember we are all wonderful unique individuals so sometimes what works for one person may not work for another.

Having got the serious stuff out the way; the most important point to make is just go out there and let nature be your companion and let her power be a peace maker and healer to you in this busy world.

The Walk

Above; the footpath to the left from Long Rock to Jordan's Cafe which hosts a great abundance of edible coastal plants.

Contents	Page
Introduction	6-8
Let's start with Ray	9-15
Messages From Ray	16-17
Poem; Ray	18-19
Where we will forage.	20-21
Let's start foraging	22

The Plants;

	Page
Alexanders And **The Umbellifers**	23-28
Black Mustard	29
Burdock	30-31
Cleavers	32-35
Clover	36-37
Cowslip	38
Danish Scurvy Grass	39
Dandelion	40-43
Docks	44--45
Eyebright	46-47
Garlic Mustard	48
Gorse	49
Grass	50-53
Hawthorn	54-55
Herb Robert	56-58
Hogweed	59-60
Mallow	61-62
Mullein	63-64
Nettle	65-68
Pennywort	69-70
Pineapple Weed	71
Plantain	72-73
Rock Samphire	74

Rose Bay Willow Herb	75-76
SeaBeet	77-79
Sea Buckthorn	80-82
Sea Cabbage	83-84
Sea Campion	85
Sea Holly	86
Sea Radish	87
Sorrel	88-89
Sow Thistle	90-91
Thistles	92-93
Three Cornered Leek	94-95
Yarrow	96-97

Additional Plants.

Self Heal	98.
Wood Averns	99.
Lady's Mantle	100

Basic Seaweed Knowledge — **101- 106**

Extraordinary Pioneers Of The Natural World	107-110
Wild Soul	111-112
Fitzgerald Quote	113
Ray's Articles	114-127
Summary Of Healing	128-129
Further Reading And Visuals	130-132
Useful Terms In Foraging And Healing	133-136
Latin Names And Stories Behind Them	136-137
Seaweed Summary	137-138
Farewell	139-141

'A Foraging Walk For Ray,' celebrates the teachings of a man who dedicated himself to nature. Ray was a man who showed us edible treasure from the Cornish hedgerow and coastal paths; his wisdom told a story about how these plants connected us to the land and sea. He brought together the pioneers, both past and present, who echoed the importance of this connection, a voice shouting out to us about what we have lost and how we need to return to nature's great story before we systematically destroyed it. Ray was the the silken thread that stitched all these philosophies together so beautifully, to remind us who we are.

'This book is a great resource for learning plant knowledge, particularly about the edible plants that grow abundantly on The West coast of Cornwall. It also comes with some useful tips on identifying plants safely. What I really liked is the reflections throughout of the great pioneers like Rachel Carson, Dr Maynard Murray, Ann Wigmore, Masanobu Fukuoka and more recently the work of Zach Bush and how Ray linked them together as an important background to our understanding, that we are not only connected to nature but to all the elements needed for the functioning of the human body which are the sea and the plants. In other words we are nature! Ray's articles in the back of the book are a fascinating snippet of his ideas, to reinforce everything he believed and taught.'

Hi this is me above Emma. I have lived in Cornwall for 24 years now and I love it. I have two dogs, a teenage son, two step daughters and my partner Matthew. Life is good but there have been tough times. In 2015 I suffered a breakdown that lasted 2 years and on my recovery the most amazing man knocked on my door and helped me change my life. I want to share with you all the knowledge he gave me so you will never look at Cornish hedges in the same way again

'Just for a moment, I invite you to forget what you learned at School in history lessons the saga of men's efforts to control earth as their property. Consider this; the land was here before us and will outlive us. The land is not inanimate, it owns us, and we are just some of these creatures. The land lends us minerals, feeds us, clothes us, houses us –if we have the will to work- and when we die it takes back all it has given.. people who are too arrogant to accept the land is their master parcel it up and say 'this is my farm, 'this is my forest' and they trade with us amongst themselves with the products the land has lent them. Their myths are the foundation of the society into which you and I were born..but for me it is not enough to simply visit the land. I want to accept all its gifts, spiritual and material and I want them direct- not processed or packaged by someone else and always with a price tag.'

(Anthony Wigens, The Clandestine Farm 1980 page 11 to 12.)

Dedicated to Ray Yarwood 1937 to 2024

Introduction

Let's start with Ray

Ray was my neighbour since 2011 when my son was born and we moved into the Towans at Phillack. It wasn't till 2016 after I was recovering from a terrible mental breakdown that had destroyed me for 2 years that he became an integral part of my life.

He knocked on my door and asked if I would like to learn about foraging. Ray was one of the most kind and thoughtful people I have met and this was a beautiful offering; a gift that helped me heal and so began a seven year journey of coffee, cake and one of the most fascinating , enjoyable subjects I have ever learned. Tuesday mornings were never the same. Originally a 1 hour lesson turned to 2 then 3 with trips out when the weather was good.

Mounts Bay was one of his favourite stretches. I also took him to Prussia Cove once a magical place for edible plants. We stumbled upon the famous annual Prussia Cove Music festival. Ray of course stopped and chatted to many of the international musicians taking great delight in their stories; for that was Ray he loved people. His wife Sylvia knew from their regular Thursday Botanical walks in Hayle that a 20 minute stroll soon turned into 2 hours as Ray chatted with everyone telling them the most fascinating facts about the plants along there; he gave' the head Gardener advice on gardening without chemicals' as to his dismay (and mine) he was still using Roundup!

Sylvia was always helping us with the photocopying and admin for these lessons but her jaw was always dropping every week at yet another delivery driver that would turn up with another book he had ordered around the subject of plants and nature.

He gifted me his books when he passed; there are too many to read for Ray's brain was astonishing. Ray's presence was healing, he was a story teller, a profit, a teacher and an educator; he knew where we were heading on this planet and in a way he was preparing us; but preparing us in 'his' way with complete gentleness, humility and kindness.

He was an amazing writer and as well as writing fiction novels he wrote articles that used to bring some of the greatest pioneers of the natural world together, like Rachel Carson, Theo Coleburn, Zach Bush, Masanobu Fukuoka and Dr Maynard Murray and he would connect their words and landscape of thoughts, creating beautiful analogies in articles that were sharp and intelligent, and for the most part under-valued by the majority of the local rag's viewers.

As well as Coleburn and Bush's work, Ray knew that Fitzgerald's 'The Hundred Year Lie' and 'Swallow This,' strategically were warning us that chemicals were not serving the human body and spirit. From the 1930s onwards there was an obvious exponential rise in autoimmune conditions within children; you see Ray was brought up in the war and as a little tot had scrambled into bunkers only to listen to the mighty bombs destroying his town outside; yet during those times, he always used to comment that despite the smog from the burning coal industries, certain health outcomes were better; only one person in his class would be known to have an ailment such as asthma or autism. It was of no coincidence that during the war people had access to growing their own vegetables and Ray thought this along with other factors was a significant in reflecting these trends. You can go as far down the 'rabbit hole, as you wish to with this but some of those rabbit holes may or may not reveal light in the end and it is up to you to educate yourself and decide what is your truth? Since Ray's childhood the increase and expectation of children to have more and more contact with chemicals and processed food, would correlate with poorer health outcomes; a fact that the big industries making profit from this would do their best to cover up.

Many pioneers were writing about this but were often being drowned out by mainstream journalism. Both Zach Bush and Beth Lambert particularly in her book 'A Compromised Generation' were shouting loudly that the chemicals in our blood, our digestive systems and in the atmosphere were taking a toll on our bodies and that of our offspring. Ray knew food, the food industry and the pursuit of profit in big Pharma was one of the wars we were facing today.

He talked very often of Dr Maynard Murray (see extraordinary pioneers'at the end) who studied sea animals and found no disease or disparity in cellular health between Mother and offspring especially compared with river fish who were often struck so easily with disease. Murray scientifically explains the great power of the sea to cleanse and heal itself and the land around it. When storms came in they would feed the plants and trees with the rich array of minerals from the sea. Only Ray could have spoken of a hurricane and storms with such joy and passion.

He understood that living where he and Sylvia lived connected them every day with this great source. His garden around his house was originally flat and sandy and he created a wild heaven by wheel barrowing seaweed back from the beach to build his soil and what a landscape he built! Plants from all around the world that provided both shelter and food.

Ray's forest garden was a point of interest to many gardeners who were gifted with cuttings. It is nice to think his green off-springs were reproducing around the county.

What Ray gave to me was a gift of sustainability to use for the rest of my life. If the world went down tomorrow I could happily eat from the hedge and so could my 12 year old son who cited 30 edible plants from his head the other day and that was all because of Ray, who also used to deliver Seb fruit leathers he had painstakingly made from his sea buckthorn berries and apples that grew so bountiful in his garden.

Animals loved Ray ..the ex-battery chickens he owned used to run to him for a cuddle. I have tried this with my chickens but they run away! My dogs would sit around him when he visited on a Tuesday; Tarka's head in his lap whilst he recited some of the most fascinating facts to all of us,including my Mom who would nod off in the back chair.

A close friend of mine who had the ability to 'see ghosts' claimed that she saw 'mythical nature sprites' all around Ray once when she met him in his forest garden. It was a surprise to her as well she had never seen them before and didn't know they existed.

Sometimes my mind would totally connect with Ray in between our weekly meetings..I once bought some tuning forks and was learning about sound healing. Before our lesson, I was driving back from my son's School and was listening to a podcast from a sound healer called Eileen McClusik ... Later that morning when Ray arrived, even though it was nothing to do with foraging, I showed him my tuning forks, he was fascinated and surprised me by pulling out Eileen McClusik's book which he had ordered that very week. He then gifted me the book as he said it was obviously meant to be.

Ray thought wild plants were the answer to our healing and he himself ate 15 different wild leaves a day. This was our way to gaining back our own empowerment and our health.

Some of his ideas were scoffed at, like walking bare foot or wearing leather soled shoes so we could connect and disperse our positive ions back into the Earth and now all proven in studies in the new edition of 'Earthing' or the original pioneer book 'The invisible Rainbow,' about how we are electrical beings.

These books along with numerous other studies and insights from ESUK, also backed his opinion on 5G; despite writing to his local MP with his concerns he always received a disheartening robotic response stating how the UK would be at the forefront of technology. Ray knew the politicians no longer worked for the people and many a Tuesday he would shed a tear when talking about the losses of children and the young to the wars around the planet.

In spring Ray always said it's not 'Counting your blessing,' **It's counting your Blossom.'** He said it in such a playful way; no wonder children and animals were drawn to him.

Last year (2023) the Hawthorn and the plum tree outside my door were the most beautiful blossom I have ever seen and perhaps they were honouring one of the most beautiful lives.

Ray died quietly and quickly in January this year (2024) and on the day he died the sky was clear and he sat in his forest garden for the last time and felt the sun on his face. I couldn't have wished for a quicker passing for he had talked to me about death many times. One of his favourite pioneers Dr Zach Bush, who worked in end of life care, had described the utter horror of patients who had passed away, only to be brought back to life and had always said 'Why did you bring me back?' Ray wanted to leave this world quickly. It was his 87th year. If his body was as sharp as his mind I really believed he had a lot more years but there were circumstances that I believe compromised his health. (see the poem Wild Soul at the end.)

Sometimes I used to film Ray's lessons and I couldn't find them after he died until they turned up randomly on one of my old laptops when I plugged it in, to my surprise there they were 14 sessions as well as other little clips..us laughing and joking and collecting from the hedge. I will be editing and sharing all.

Playing them brings the beautiful peace and presence of Ray into the room. Please go to **'Raymond's Wisdom'** on You Tube to watch these and you will really pick up his warming presence too. Ray also created his own website way before I met him called **'Towan's Forest Garden.'**

Perhaps we can have a special place for people to access this knowledge in all the books he had read; for Ray's head was a library; a library that questions the harsh destructive practices that were diminishing the light of our existent and he held this light so magically.

Through the foraging walks mainly along Mount's Bay, this book, his website and my YouTube channel I hope Ray's teachings are able to spread, influence and warm the hearts of many whilst we transition into a new world with many challenges ahead. May we all get back to working alongside, and not against, the great power of nature where Ray somewhere, in its ether currently resides.

One of the last books he gave me to read was Anthony Wigens, 'The Clandestine Farm,' in which he states;

'The land lends us minerals, feeds us, clothes us, houses us ....and when we die it takes back all it has given..'

One of the last plants we talked about was The Lesser Celandine of which he leant me a poem about this special flower by Dorothy Wordsworth. The other day on a path I had taken by accident, I noticed that unusually, it was littered with Lesser Celandine, some were in flower and this time I was so sure that Ray has just departed his body only and he will be around all of us.

In fact I keep seeing this flower and the picture at the beginning of me was on a walk along from Zennor where I took the wrong turn and ended up in a field of Lesser Celandine; which I have never seen in my life! Believe what you want but I think if we open our hearts we can feel our departed all around us, *for like nature we are all part of a cycle that renews itself and is forever connected to its source.*

Sylvia Ray's wife, Martin his son, all who loved him will take a part of Ray in their hearts, for like the Lesser Celandine its modest name does not really impart its stunning hopeful appearance in spring and its medicinal and healing qualities it brings to us. In fact most plants have been forgotten and undermined on purpose because they lead us 'mere' humans to our awakening that we are not 'mere.' Plants are powerful tools that show us so much healing and magic and Ray was one of the pioneers that came to this planet to show us just that.

Thank you Ray; Thank you for this walk and this book you helped me write.

'Pansies Lillies, Kingcups, Daisies

Let them live upon their prairies

Long as there's a sun that sets

Primroses will have their glory

Long as there are Violets

They will have a place in story

There's a flower that shall be mine

Tis The Little Celandine.'

(Dorothy Wordsworth)

Above; Me and Ray having a wonder in his beautiful forest garden 2021

MessagesFrom Ray; THE MOST IMPORTANT PART OF THIS BOOK

I had nearly finished this book and I felt there was something missing. This book is about a walk, I originally thought it was a foraging walk to give basic knowledge; but it is more than that, it is introducing you to the connection we have to the sea and the land around us and **the messages this extraordinary man delivered me to deliver you**. So whilst the plant profiles are easy to understand you will not understand their real magic if I don't share with you why Ray came to this conclusion. The heroes such as Ann Wigmore, Rachel Carson, Dr Maynard Murray and more recently Zach Bush were and are all profits of the modern age delivering a simple Psalm. **Ray was the alchemist who connected them all**. Sharing their books at the end is not enough. What I really need to share is some of the articles and letters Ray wrote. Some were scoffed at but **now I look at them and realise they are integral to our next steps on this journey to retrieve what has been so purposefully taken from us; which is our connection to nature.**

So I started to rifle through my cupboards for the photocopies he had given me with a view to sharing a couple of articles but then I found many; just like The Lesser Celandine that had communicated itself to me when he died.

All articles were so eloquently written; simple intelligent messages for humanity. What was astonishing was the two subjects he wrote about the most was 'Mother Sea,' and 'Grass' not only the connection to each other but their ability to heal and when you read my section on Grass you will understand the connection it has to the sea; both elements supporting us by holding around 90 minerals to give access, not just to survive but to thrive in such a beautiful way

Dr Maynard Murray in the book Fertility From The Ocean Deep,' talks about this in depth (excuse the pun.) My original idea was to share 1 or 2 of Ray's articles but I realised that I needed to share as many of Ray's letters that I could find and despite them being at the back of the book I have to say they are the most important part of it. So once you have brought plants into your life to enhance and improve your health, your energy and your happiness; put rocket fuel onto that and read Ray's letters / articles. You will never look back; There are repetitions but Ray did that to instil knowledge in people just as the media and the government have programmed you to disconnect from nature and the power it has to rejuvenate the human spirit.

Enjoy this book and I hope it starts you on a path to a new life with better health and more energy.

Ray

Ray, my dear ray has gone away

It only seems like yesterday

When his soft tones

Filled room and granite

A message of hope about our planet.

A man bright with stories and kindness, now rarely seen

A brief case of books and himself, no wifi, mobile or any screen.

For Ray, he loved the Cornish air,

The rich minerals of the sea, the hedgerow plants all free to share.

In his younger days he pushed weed of the sea in his barrow,

He knew it was no weed, it built his soil and grew his marrow.

From sand to dirt he planted plants and trees from around the world

And gardeners would gather in this space to hear his word.

And there his message was beautiful and clear

We can build this earth again for we have everything here.

Em (2024)

Above. Ray's barrow that he used to bring back full of seaweed to his garden, in order to build quality soil on sand dunes.

Where will we Forage?

My first walk is along Mount's Bay specifically from Long Rock Car park which is before Morrison's Penzance and just before Long Rock Industrial estate you turn left and cross over the railway lines to park.

On foot we head North towards Marazion and wander along looking at the vast varieties of plants here. Known as the 'Fertile Mile,' this stretch had a reputation for producing nutritious agricultural vegetables which benefited from the minerals evaporating from the sea and also the Seaweed that was collected regularly to be dried and fed to the soil as fertiliser. This was exactly the same way that Ray created his Forest garden by wheel-barrowing seaweed from St Ives Bay.

PREPARING FOR FARMS AROUND MOUNT'S BAY-'FERTILE MILE'

Above; Post war communities helping to load seaweed onto a trailer to use as fertiliser on the soil that was to be known as the 'Golden Mile,' or 'Fertile Mile.'

Above an artist's portrayal (unknown) of the carts on Marazion beach picking up free fertiliser in the form of seaweed. One of Ray's favourite pictures.

Let's start foraging!

Things To Remember; Firstly read The Disclaimer on page 2

1. **Basically; Respect, protect and don't take any risks be 110% sure before you pick and eat. If in doubt leave it out.**

2. Any new edibles you decide to taste, just go for a tiny amount; remember you have not experienced this plant before so just because it is edible doesn't mean it will suit you.

3. Don't pick endangered species and harvest according to that plant's needs. If you take the root of a plant you are supposed to ask the land owner's permission.

4. Harford says Foragers are some of the 'most ecologically deeply embedded in their environment,' and therefore **'you don't destroy what you love**.' These plants are always so around **pick less, fresh and often,** giving them chance to grow back.

5. Our aim always to keep the heritage of plants alive or even renew their uses both nutritionally and medicinally.

6. The plant world is huge but my job is to introduce you to a few in your local environment that will provide nutrition and potential healing to use in your everyday life.

7. **Always trace a plant down its stem with your hands to make sure you are picking the right leaf, Hemlock can grow in the hedge amongst Herb Robert and Three Cornred Leek grows next to Bluebell. They all look similar but; take your time picking plants is a beautiful process.**

The Plants (In Alphabetical order with Seaweed at the end)

Alexanders (Syrnium Olusatrum)Horse Parsley

Umbelliferae family (same family as Hemlock.)

The coast is 'littered with Alexanders.'

Its story; Known as *'Parsley of The Romans'* who were thought to have brought it here. The horses were also fond of this abundant plant hence it's name 'Horse Parsley.'

Replaced by celery around the 17thcentury. Often was used in pottage with nettles and watercress and in the Hebredes cooked with Lamb to fight consumption.

History records that *Queen Elizabeth had Alexanders with fish.*

Everyday food; I eat the leaves in salad and chop up stalks like celery on newly sprouted stems but we can eat all the plant; seeds both green then black can be ground for spice and used in place of pepper.

Roots can be boiled with oil and vinegar served like parsnip too. Leaves have a slightly tangy taste with a celery edge to them and are **great for stomach complaints.**

I make a spicy tomato soup. Add butter, garlic, sea salt, garlic, Bullion, onions and tomatoes.

Try the leaves in a white sauce or even use in ice cream like Alice from the Goose Barn (nr Gweek) has done.

Used for mouth sores in cattle scurvy, which doesn't surprise me because chewing on Alexander makes your mouth feel super fresh!

Flowers can be pickled and fried in batter or used in place of broccoli as cooking will lose some of its aromatic flavour in cooking.

Hugh Fearnley made a liquor out of Alexanders.

Medicinally; The strong taste of Alexanders proves to be warming and purging for the bowls, a diuretic for the bladder they have antiseptic actions and are a great digestive tonic, blood cleanser, stomach strengthener, and they reduce inflammation.

Sailors used to go ashore to collect Alexanders to prevent Scurvy due to its **high its Vit C content.**

In Moncriet 18th century book..***Poor Man's Physician***, *Alexanders were prescribed for* swollen tissues and stopping febrile convulsions.

Culpeper (1616-1654) describes Alexanders as able to 'move women's courses' and expel afterbirth.

The Biologically active component called **isofuranodiene** in Alexanders have shown **inhibits the growth of colon, uterine and breast cancer,** enhancing chemo treatments. (Maggi) 2014.

An ancient remedy from 15th century put Alexander seeds, Sage, Sow Thistle seeds, Betony (leaves and roots), made into a powdered cake with ale was said to heal the sick.

No known contraindications but exercise precaution when breast feeding or pregnant.

Differences with Hemlock and other Umbellifers

N.B, Both Alexanders and Hogweed (see Hogweed) have a very different shape to Hemlock so I do pick these but I don't tend to pick the Wild Chervil family with 'feathery' Hemlock leaves. There are a few Wild Chervils but Wild Carrot often has a small pink flower in the middle and Cow Parsley (Queen's Anne's is Lace another name for it) both have hairy and ridged stems. Hemlock is very smooth and rounded and often has purple blotches on like it has been flicked with a paint brush. Hemlock stems also smell like Acetone or nail varnish; so use all your senses to identify plants BUT with this family I would generally avoid picking unless you are super confident.

Refer to picture of this family in the Herb Robert section which has similar shape leaves but are positioned at the end of the stem in a half star or heart shape and their stems and leaves redden up later on.

Water Hemlock Dropwort (which looks quite celery like), has a lovely smell. **Both are deadly** particularly Hemlock which causes paralysis from the leg upwards until it reaches the mouth and causes a muscular grin known as the '*sardonic grin,*' a method used to kill prisoners of war in Sardinia.

Hemlock Dropwort requires immediate hospital visit and can affect the heart **so be absolutely sure you know these two plants visually. Dropwort could be compared to Alexanders** but it tends to grow by rivers in its masses..you will learn to recognise the difference.

Whilst Hemlock has feathery type leaves,' Alexander's are more oval and have serrated edges.

IF IN DOUBT LEAVE IT OUT (see pictures on next 3 pages.)

Above; Top of picture Hemlock Water Dropwort leaves. This plant is highly poisonous and grows mainly by rivers and can grow near to Alexanders . The bottom right half of picture shows Alexander leaves which ar e bigger and have a very different shape more rounded with serrated edges . If in doubt do not pick.

Above; Hemlock Water Dropwort (St Erth canal) Looks very 'Celery like,' and grows by rivers. This is highly toxic and does not have any medicinal use despite the 'Wort' in its name as Dropwort this is possibly a reference to the shape of the tubers on its root although many poisonous plant can still be used medicinally in tiny amounts in the past. Also known as Dead Man's Fingers. There are many edible versions in the Carrot family but I mainly avoid them to save fatal errors.

Above; Galloway Wild Foods shows us the striking similarities between Hemlock (left) and Wild Parsley (Queen's Anne's Lace) Right..it is probably not worth the risk. Note Wild parsley stems are hairy and ridged whereas Hemlock is smooth with purple blotches but I myself don't bother foraging this plant the result of error is too great.

Black Mustard (Brassica nigra)

Its Story; You can't miss this beautiful plant; it as rough leaves and sometimes purple stems. Beautiful yellow flowers with four petals typical of the Cruciferous (cross/4 parts) family, which includes Sea Cabbage and Sea Radish. May have come from The East or Med & to Britain around 1720.

Everyday food; Put in salads if you can handle heat or just add to hot dishes curries to reduce the heat and enjoy the taste.

Medicinally; Chest colds, bronchial infections and a great detoxer. Seeds used to be crushed and put directly onto chests. Specifically**; Omega 3 and 6, fatty acids, Potassium, Calcium and Phosphorous and a great antioxidant.**

Above; Beautiful array of Black Mustard in flower which show a soft yellow haze in hedgerows and field around the coast.

Burdock (*Arctium minus.*) *Stickleburr, Velcro Plant.*

Asteraceae family (Daisy). Biennial.

Other varieties; Artium Lappa; 'Greater,' which is huge or Tomentosum; Woolly Burdock which is more grey.

You may not see this on Ray's walk but it is affluent in certain areas like **Perranuthnoe** and you can't miss its beautiful heart shape gigantic leaves.

Its story; Burdock was the reason **Velcrose** was invented from the burrs that stick to you. The inventor George de Mestral a Swiss Engineer, noticed the burs sticking to his clothes after a walk and spent two decades studying them to reproduce a synthetic version.

Burdock's Stems are hollow turning from green to red.

Everyday food; The Root is the most popular called gobo by The Japanese..contains the most nutrients; chop and fry to make Burdock chips.

Roots should be picked in the first year when they are more nutritious and as leaves die after first frost, you may need to mark the plant with a stick to establish how old it is.

The second year all the energy goes into the flowers but the **leaf** can be picked in early spring. Add early spring leaves to salad or boil/cook and don't forget you can make a Dandelion and Burdock drink.

Medicinally; Burdock's are excellent sources of multiple Bs(2,3,5,6) and vitamins especially C,E and K. Also rich in Managanese, Phosphorus, Choline, Calcium, Iron, Copper and Selenium.

Burdock cleanses and purifies; make teas or tincture. It has been used to treat gout, constipation, stomach disorders and an alternative cancer treatment globally to get rid of tumours (Hildegard Of Bingen.) This comes from the arctigenin found in the root which has anti tumour, anti inflammatory, anti viral and anti oxidant qualities.

The whole plant cleanses the blood and removes toxins.

Above; Big beautiful Burdock leaves

Above; Lesser Burdock's 'thistle like' burs (both Wildcornwall.com)

Cleavers (Gallium aparine) Sticky Weed, Goose Grass.

You cannot fail to identify this great plant as it sticks to your clothes; always abundant in the spring. It can be confused however with Hedge Bedstraw (see pic). Cleavers like Hedge Bedstraw, can also have purple stripes on their stem when they start to reach maturity

Its Story; Named *Galium aparine* from the family Rubiaceae referring to red dye produced from its roots.

Cleaver's also known as *Stickyweed, Goose Grass* as Geese love it but horse, cows and sheep love it too.

Gallium is Greek for milk.. referring to this group of plant's ability to curdle milk. Also used by Shepherds to strain milk. Can be juiced to make a vegetable rennet to curdle cheese.

Aparine is from the Greek word Aparo..to seize referring to its ability to attach itself to a person! (Linnaeus 1700s)

Cleavers are known in folklore as **the plants of connection** to cleanse yourself and create better connections through good health with people and animals.

Same family as the Bedstraws that were used as part of a mattress filler to relax people and keep fleas at bay (e.g Hedge Bedstraw and Lady Bedstraw see picture below.)

Cleaver is part of The Coffee family and one of the first shows of spring. This astringent and bitter plant is described in 'A discourse in Sallets' (John Evelyn) , as making fat people thin by mashing in with a quarter sea water then taken daily for 9 weeks and it is *'wonderful how healthy you will become!"*

Everyday food; Roots are red and a dye can be made from them. The seeds can be roasted to make a wild coffee; known as poor man's coffee because of the effort made to make it!

As a spring tonic and **lymphatic pipe cleaners** as Julia Bruton Searle describes in her amazing book 'Hedgerow Medicine' infuse in water or add to soup salads, poultice, **be careful the hairs can irritate some!**

Medicinally; Cleavers have astringent actions, they are bitter, cooling, drying and rejuvenating. Cleavers strengthen and purify the blood, they are great for fatigue, sluggish immune systems.

Gypsies have used Cleavers to treat cancer, rheumatism. Irish folk records also show its uses for tumours, inflamed bowls and stomach ache, it also eliminates excess fluid so great for **Glandular Fever and Tonsilitis**.

Native Americans used it for **infections, kidney and urinary ailments.**

The BMJ 1881 reported its pulp applied to bed ulcers which were reduced by 50% over a month.

Dr Tuthilll Massey recommended a poultice and a decoction for 6 to 12 months and Dr Thornton (Herbal 1810) after surgeon's failed to remove tumours, ordered the juice of cleavers mixed with linseeds to be applied and a teaspoon of fresh juice taken every morning with daily fasting to disperse 'frightful tumors. (Quelch 41)

Culpeper (17th century) describes it as a blood cleanse and liver strengthener.

Known to treat Jaundice In Himalayan regions and Gonohrea in the East Indies.

In a 1980 trial it was used as a tea to treat tongue cancer, throat cancer, **Goitre and Thyroid issues**.

Can counteract any skin irritation, bites, bumps, Eczema. Psoriasis, Rosaea.

In ' Plants For The People' Verinder describes The Cleaver as having 'An Impressive lymphatic tonifier with the ability to speak directly to the glandular congestion, cleavers are a prime remedy for shifting swollen glands and nodes.'

Above; Lower corner right two cleavers grow amongst Hedge bedstraw (Galium alba) which can look quite similar and are from the same family they were used as a sedative and relaxant and to stuff bedding to keep fleas at bay. Both plants edible. HB is not sticky though!

Above; Cleavers grow in abundance I would personally never rip these out of my garden they are literally spring life savers! Above show them flourishing in the hedgerow at Zennor before they flower..

Clover and Red Clover. (Trifolium repens; white, Trifolium pratens; red.)

Its story; From the Legume family Fabacea

All clovers are edible and all nitrogen fixers meaning they take nutrients from the air and water and put it into the soil.

Masanobu Fukuoka (One Straw Revolution), the guru of natural farming used Clover as an essential part of his farming process to improve soil.

Nutrients to plants is also helped through; Mycellium; Physical body of the fungus above ground and **Mycorrhizae** which *Literally translates to "fungus-root." Mycorrhiza defines as a mutually beneficial relationship between the root of a plant and a fungus that colonizes the plant root. In many plants, Mycorrhiza are fungi that grow inside the plant's roots, or on the surfaces of the roots. The plant and the fungus have a mutually beneficial relationship, where the fungus facilitates water and nutrient uptake in the plant, and the plant provides food and nutrients created by photosynthesis to the fungus. This exchange is a significant factor in nutrient cycles and the ecology, evolution, and physiology of plants.' (biologydictionary.net.) Watch 'Fantastic Fungi' on Netflix to see this powerful magic within our soil and follow the works of Paul Stamets who is instrumental in showing us the power of nature and how we can change the world.*

Everyday food; Put the leaves and flowers in salads for a delicious nutritional addition.

Medicinally; Red Clover is an astringent and full of **Iron; the flower head are the medicinal part** but you can eat all the plant above ground.

Also contains, Copper, Manganese, Selenium, Vit B and C, Bioflavonoids, Isoflavones and Inositol making it a great immune builder and detoxifier.

Great for respiratory issues and skin complaints. Isoflavones effect (type of Phytoestrogen) which can calm menopausal symptoms including hot flushes, night sweats and low mood.

Both White and Red Clover are high in proteins, vitamins and minerals and have been used for fevers, coughs and sore eyes.

Above; As Nitrogen fixers the abundant Clovers are beneficial not only to us but the soil it replenishes.

Cowslip *(Primula veris) Primula, Fairy Cups.*

Its Story; I wasn't going to put Cowslips in this book but I keep seeing small areas of it growing on the dunes; yet at one point in history it was over picked and barely any was left. It was picked to make a wine or tea that was used as a sedative helping people sleep putting them in a 'relaxed state.'

May have been called Cowslip because it grew in meadows where Cow's manure lay hence 'Cowslip!'

Everyday Food; Use the flowers to make a syrup or put in salads or on cakes. A few leaves can go into a salad but they are quite bitter so balance out with refreshing Sow Thistle and Fennel for example.

Medicinally; A diuretic and an expectorant but revered for its sedative qualities and given to over active children.

Historically has been used to treat cramps, paralysis and rheumatic pains.

Cowslip syrup is used for asthma and breathing disorders and it is a good remedy to clear catarrh.

Above; Cowslips at Gwithian Towans.

Danish Scurvy Grass (Cochlearia danica.)

Its story; Low lying almost succulent looking plant amongst the sea beet and Plantain. When Botany first became written about 'Scurvy grasses' were mentioned a lot. Roman soldiers were taught about its value when they were fighting.

Scurvy grass has heart shaped leaves which develop extra corners and turn in a rectangle shape. They are from the Brassica family and have those 'cruciferous ' four petals that are are white to pink.

Everyday food use; Has a lovely spicy mustard/ horseradish taste and can be put into salads or added to hot dishes.

Medicinally; The clue is in its name 'Scurvy Grass,' because it has a high Vitamin C content so was used, particularly by sea folk, to cure scurvy. It also has an array of minerals and vitamins typical to the Brassica family.

Above Danish Scurvy Grass at Longrock. Eat the flowers and pods.

Dandelion (*Tararxacum officinale.*)

Its story; Taraxacum refers to 'many disorders' for which Dandelion is a cure.

Also known as **Dente-de-Lion** (Lion's teeth because of it jagged edges.) Many members of this family include Sow Thistle, Cat's Ear, Prickly Ox Tongue, which you may notice on the walk and are all edible.

In Folklore Dandelion is a special plant because it represents the sun with its flower, the moon with its globe feathered seeds and the stars when the seeds are blown and scattered, and they will carry up to 5 miles.

'A mineral dense plant that replenishes depleted soil and depleted people.' ('Plants For The People. ')

The deep roots of the Dandelion brings up nutrients to the surface such as Calcium and Nitrogen.

Dandelions are used globally as a tonic and to prevent stagnation. This is due to its diuretic actions that cleanses kidneys and open the urinary tract hence its referred to as *'Piss-en-lit' in French or 'Piss The Bed!*

Collect roots in Autumn when they are the largest.

Euell Gibbons in the 60s paid tribute to the Dandelion; he reflects how thousands have been saved from winter borne illnesses through the action of harvesting the dandelions root, washing and then expressing its juice. He also mentions a community in Minorca who were saved from famine by harvesting the roots, which are more nutritious than potatoes.

According to *Family Foraging kitchen* in Devon the more sharper the point on the leaves the less bitter the plant. Rounder ones are better for cooking. The most bitter part of the leaf is the middle.

Everyday Food; Roots of the Dandelion can be shaved into coleslaw or used to make a beverage. Collect the roots in Autumn where its energy is stored, Spring and Summer are better for the leaves and flowers.

Dandelions leaves and flowers are great in salads or curries but use 'The Ultimate Dandelion Medicine Book,' to get amazing recipes from vinegar, coffee, honey to capsules and tinctures from this fabulous versatile nutritious plant (see book list.)

Flower head can be fried and stalk used as noodles or 'doodles.'

Medicinally; Dandelions are great for skin complaints like eczema, acne and psoriasis.

The Sap inside the stem will zap warts, verrucas, pimples and insect bites. Apply daily for a week.

Great for women's health and menopause.

Successful trials have used Dandelion leaf tea for Long Covid or Chronic Fatigue. The Leaf also clears fluid in bladder and kidney infections.

Personally I make an Immunity tincture by soaking Dandelions, Nettles, Cleavers in Vodka for two to 4 weeks then drain the liquid and use as a tincture over the winter. Take a tsp 3 times a day at the first sign of a cold. Take 1 tsp a day for prevention.

Unlike **Pharmaceutical diuretics which deplete Potassium** with their actions, Dandelion replenishes potassium in the body whilst cleansing the body at the same time.

Culpepper describes it as good for eyesight, a fact that his enemies the College of Physicians kept from everyone in order for them to buy their expensive potions.

Roots of Dandelions are amazing for the liver and supports emotions connected to the liver like anger, repressed feelings and rage. (Plants For The People) and the root has shown in tests to reduce the growth of cancer.

The plant's make up can cause the gall bladder to contract to produce bile, it then stimulates the liver to produce more. As well as this it is great for the pancreas so an all round digestive marvel.

Dandelions are High in Potassium and Vitamins A and C ,K , E and an arrays of Bs (1,2,5,6,9 and 12) ,Calcium, Magnesium, Iron , Potassium, Phosphorus, Copper, Manganese and Zinc. This amazing plant also has powerful antioxidants such as Beta-Carotene and Polyphenols, Sodium, Choline Lecithin, Biotin and Inositol. It is high in protein and contains 8 amino acids!

Katrina Blair in her book 'The Wild Wisdom Of weeds,' compares the amount of Beta-Carotene, Calcium, Iron and Potassium in Dandelion leaves to lettuce and carrots which showed Dandelions to have 7000 units per ounce, lettuce 1200 per ounce and carrots 1275!

Summary; One of the best plants nutritionally the other two are Nettles and Grass with Cleavers coming in at a close second (in my opinion of course!)

Above; My favourite inland hedge foraging books ..the Seal family chose the Dandelion as its cover. Like the awesome nettle most foragers adore and are in awe of The Dandelion and its powers to heal. I bought this book for Ray and he loved it!

Dock (*Rumex obtusifolius*)

Or **Rumex crispus;** curly docks, both native to Britain and Ireland.

Its story; Docks are from the Buckwheat family, so similar to cabbage or spinach and so cooked that way. **You can use Kelp or Dock as a layer instead of pasta or between pasta layers.**

Like Dandelion they are very tough and will survive anything. In 'Knowledge To Forage,' they claim that studies of this plant shows it to be able to survive under water for eight weeks!

The dock is capable of producing thousands of seeds which are known to survive for 50 years in undisturbed soil! The seeds are also essential for many birds, deer and rodents.

Although there is mixed bag of opinions in the foraging world about this bitter hedge plant which has mainly been promoted as a sting pacifier. The modest Dock actually holds great nutrients and should be eaten, however is not particularly effective with nettle stings!

The sting myth; At the bottom of Dock leaf in the stalk is a sticky sap 'the mucalage;' and this part of the dock is what is good for easing stings. As this knowledge was passed down it has lost the essential part. In reality Plantain is much better at soothing stings and bites. Other soothers are Chickweed and Daisy.

Everyday food; Stems can be chopped sweetened and used instead of rhubarb and the seeds can be boiled or ground and added to flour.

Vix who is part of the *Family Foraging Kitchen at Rame,* rates it as one of her favourite plants because of its high Iron content and other nutrients she uses it as spinach or tops lasagnes with it. I have tried this and it is lovely.

Medicinally; Studies show Docks rich in both proteins, carbohydrates, flavanoids and antioxidants. Docks are very high in Vitamin A and C as well as B1 and B2. **The Dock contains more Iron than cabbage.**

In first aid you can use a Dock as a bandage with Plantain or Yarrow underneath.

Seeds used for coughs and colds and roots for jaundice, liver problems, rheumatism, constipation and diarrhoea.

Like Sorrel it contains Oxalic Acid which shouldn't be used in excess.

Above; Broadleaf Dock on the Helford River.

Eyebright (*Euphrasia officinalis)* 'Fairy flax, Christ's Eyes, Bird's Eye, Joy Flower.

Its Story; We may not see this at Longrock today but it is often carpeted across the dunes; tiny flower we often tread on flowering from July to September. I Love this plant on a sensory level I sense it is powerful.

Eyebright needs another grass or plant it is half parasitic so needs to attach to its neighbours roots. If it gets nutrients from grass we know it is good.

Very beautiful to look at and with a name like Eyebright, surprisingly very useful for eye problems. A white flower with yellow eyes and about 2cm high.

Culpeper called it **'the flower of the sun.'** He also said if it was used as much as it is neglected it would spoil the spectacles trade! **In France it is known as Casse-Lunnette (Spectacle Breaker.)** It is well documented in Medieval times.

Carrying Eyebright in ones pockets was supposed to enhance their psychic abilities and help people understand who was telling the truth hence its other names 'Christ Sight,' and Christ's Eyes.'

Everyday food; Dry out and store; soak in water overnight to use as an eye bath for you and your pets.

Soak in vodka for two weeks then strain; use to make a health tincture to prevent colds or use as an anti-histamine to help reduce hay fever symptoms.

Make a tea with two teaspoons of the leaves and flowers.

Medicinally; Benefits include restoring vision, reducing inflammation, applied to childen's eyes during Measles to prevent later problems.

Has anti inflammatory, antiseptic actions from its content of caffeic acid. Its Tannin content helps dry up the eyes as an astringent and relieve inflammation so also great for clearing mucus.

Above; Stunning and underrated, the little Eyebright Flower. Enlarged about 3cm high (including Stem)normally.

Garlic Mustard (Alliaria petiolata)

Its Story; Traditionally known at 'Jack By The Hedge,' one of the oldest spices dates back 6000 years. Again from the *Brassica family so look out for the four petals.*

The Europeans introduced it to North America where it is now considered a pest but great food for the Green Veined Butterfly.

The leaves start shooting and grow into a kidney shape, followed by a heart shape leaf with little rounded edges. It has small white flowers very beautiful to look at and even more surprising when tasted.

Everyday food; Make a great pesto, add to soups and salads or make a Mustard sauce with the leaves.

Medicinally; Has more Vitamin C than an orange and is a great disinfectant so can help clear infection.

Above just outside my house I am seeing this more and more.

Gorse (*Ulex europaeus.*)

Its Story From the pea family was used as a symbol of fertility in weddings.

There are always Gorse flowers throughout the year as the saying goes *'When the Gorse flowers stop, kissing is out of fashion.'*

We often take Gorse for granted as it does spread and we treat it like a weed, but the great Swedish botanist Linnaus, who created the universal Latin index, fell to his feet at the sight of it in 1736.

Everyday Food; Add flowers to salad, dry them out for a calming tea.

Medicinally; Has been used for depression and is very high in Vitamin C.

In Irish folk medicine, it was widely used to treat coughs, colds, sore throats, Consumption (Tuberculosis), asthma, heartburn, hiccups, Jaundice, heart problems, dermatitis, ringworm, swellings, and as a general tonic.

Above; Gorse flower; Steeple Lane St Ives with its rich array of yellow flavoursome flowers.

Grass. *(Poaceae family ;this has 10000 species!)*

The amazing story of Grass; read Ray's letters, he loved Grass!

The Connection between Sea and Grass (All Varieties)

Its story; Grasses *'As a survival food could save your asses.'* Katrina Blair

Ray often wrote that we are exactly the same as plants in our capture of energy from the sun using photosynthesis; the only difference is we use Fe(Iron) and a plant uses Mg (Magnesium.) Grass is one of the most nutritious plants. Grasses have survived and developed for thousands of years and I can't tell you about grass without telling you about Ann Wigmore, one of Ray's favourite pioneers in the natural world. She eventually set up **Hippocrates**, the movement for Natural Health, in the U.S.A.

Ann Wigmore (her biography is called 'Why Suffer') was from Eastern Lithuania 1916 and at the age of seven was herding sheep on her own after taking the place of her friend Hilda who was murdered by marauders.

Ann was the real life Snow White of Lithuania; very connected to animals. Her stories find us in a harsh environment for a 7 year old but they are also heartening in the way that the animals became her friends and protectors.

During winter Ann's Grandmother, the local healer, used to dip Ann in a warm swamp mud bath for hours to absorb and benefit from the minerals it brought up from the earth. She also did it for her older patients to ease their rheumatic pains. Most would find the experience relaxing and often fall asleep.

One day Ann fell asleep but soon she was awoken by a bull frog on her face, croaking very loudly .. she noticed the swamp had unusually risen and was at her ears; she was about to drown. She got out and ran back to her Grandmother's only to discover a great flood swept the garden minutes later. That day her Grandmother explained that the bullfrog had saved her life.

Her Grandmother's healing techniques were interesting and effective; for coughs she would wrap her in matted wool skin for 3 days as the sheep's oil would heal and ease the lungs. She cured a mutilated arm with Rye-straw and ground Grass soaked in goat's milk.

When Ann's dog, who used to protect her as a Shepherdess, was taken by Wolves, a Crow came into her life she named Blackberry. Blackberry used to watch for strangers when Anne was herding by flying ahead and 'sqwauking' if he saw anybody coming. Blackberry was also found to be somewhat a thief when they discovered lost trinkets of the villagers in his nest!

Ann was also saved by a skunk from two thieves who approached her and were going to kill her! Lady albino (she had named her) who she used to share her lunch with, sprayed them both in the eye with her aromatic urine.

Star became her second dog from a deceased Russian soldier but Star and Blackberry humorously became enemies, both fighting for Anne's attention.

Star rescued her from quicksand by running and getting the villagers and barking after Ann fell in to the swamp one day.

After the harsh environment she had grown up in, Ann moved to the USA where her parents had gone to seek a new life. The boat journey was treacherous and sadly, her parents gave her a cold reception. This was also after the customs had cut all her beautiful long hair off claiming she had Nits, with intention to sell them on the black market of course.

Ann was surprised to find weakened bodies in the 'affluent' West and she described the people's health as *'lacking certain nutrients and were susceptible to harmful organisms.'*

After refusing to get her leg amputated after a cart accident when she was 16 she was rejected by her near society and particularly her abusive Father. Not wanting to lose her leg she remembered everything her Gran had taught her and with use of herbs and Grass and a daily lick from her puppy, the wounds healed. The Medics were baffled.

She left her parents and after an abusive marriage she eventually started a new life in Boston and based her research on a plant she knew as the most nutritious; **Grass!**

Ann knew Grass could pick up all 92 elements needed for the human body. She set a healing environment where people would come and drink grass juice. The results were miraculous severe long term health conditions and terminal cancers were cured.

Everyday food; Pick two handfuls and cut them up into 2 inch lengths and juice in a masticator with apple and Nettles OR soak in filtered water for a few hours then sieve the grass out and add lemon for a healthy tonic. Ray's recommendation *if you had a serious illness like cancer the juice would act like a transfusion and renewal of your body. Always use/soak within 2 hours of picking. Fast with this recipe In a health emergency for 2 to 4 weeks. Then introduce raw foods and build back gradually to a normal healthy diet with lots of vegetables.*

Medicinally; Grass is similar to Seawater in the array of minerals it has to offer and many books that talk about sea nutrition always link the two.

Grass juice is described as a natural transfusion or cleanser; **_Seawater was also used in this way by a French scientist called Renee Quinton who saved many lives in France in the 1930s._** It is hard to find his work as many great natural discoveries were shelved in a bid to promote Allopathic Medicine (see The Hundred Year Lie by R Fitzgerald.)

A woman who also promotes this practice from the influence of Anne Wigmore is Katrina Blair her book 'The Wild Wisdoms Of Weeds' describes how Grass binds toxins in the blood and removes them, it creates alkalinity which reduces addictive habits, and replenishes the body with minerals. Katrina delivers Grass juice on an electric milk cart to her local neighbourhood.

Grass is both anti Inflammatory and anti-bacterial.

Below; Dr Ann's books are still around and inspiring people today she became a great voice for the natural health movement in the USA, setting up Hippocrates and used grass juice to cure all ailments including terminal cancers.

Hawthorn (*Crataegus* genus)

I nearly forgot this amazing abundant native tree; Known as 'The Tree Of Life,' The Hawthorn is quite special, seeped in folklore and protected by fairies. I can only direct you to Bill Vaughn who wrote a whole book about Hawthorn and its place in history and healing. The book of course is called 'Hawthorn'

Used for centuries in marriage and ceremonies and as a fertility symbol , Hawthorn is also associated with Jesus's crown and is said to be a portal for fairies..never cut a Hawthorn tree down unless you want trouble in your life!

Everyday food; we love Hawthorn Ketchup; simmer berries and put them through the sieve add cider vinegar and sugar/ coconut sugar , salt and pepper to create the right consistency.

Make jam or chutney with the tart berries.

Eat young leaves and flowers in salad or make a tea.

Medicinally; Used by the Chinese since 659 a.d but in the USA, a man called **Greene** in the 1800s used a ' secret' formula for helping patients with heart conditions. It was revealed on his death to be Hawthorn (C.monogyna.)

This work was continued by a physician **MC Jennings** who reported many cases of curing heart conditions. It became widely used in medicine after Jenning's work along with *Digitalis* (Foxglove.)

The Eclectics a group of Physicians who started in the 1840s using herbs and individualizing treatments, took on Jennings work. They also claimed it produced a general sense of well being and this known among French peasant communities when **Maurice Messegue** used it for anxiety.

Hawthorn as a general tonic is full of **Polyphenols;** antioxidants found in plants. It does need to be taken regularly particularly the genus variety which was said not to be as strong as the American version. Making a tincture or place the berries in oil for two weeks then strain and take a few drops a day.

Overall research and clinical trials points to Hawthorn reducing blood pressure and heart rate and increasing blood flow. (Vaughn)

Other healers have said that Hawthorn can help heal Goitre, kidney and asthma and more recent research shows it improves digestion.

Research was pushed away from Medical Schools in the 1930s when chemicals came into favour (see The Hundred Year Lie R.Fitzgerald.) This doesn't allow us to resurge the benefits of Hawthorn in our everyday life.

Do not take alongside heart medicine or consult your health advisor first.

Above; Growing happily on sand the beautiful sight of Hawthorn blossom at my house.

Herb Robert, *Geranium Robertianum.*

Its story; This plant was brought to our attention by 'Julia's Edible Wild Weeds' channel (NZ) who loves this plant which is from the Geranium family (Greek for Cranesbill because the seed head is likened to a bird's beak.)

This particular species is names after Friar Robert a French Abbott known for his legendary medical skills.

Herb Robert flowers from September to May..red foliage and dark pink flowers with white stripes..stems are green to maroon. Again be careful because leaves are 'Hemlocky,' but sit very differently on the stem.

Everyday food; Recommended 5 leaves or more in smoothies, soups or teas. Julia eats one tsp spoon of dried leaf with a raw egg! It has a strong bitter and perfume taste.

Medicinally; Can be used as an insect deterrent and a deterrent in companion planting. Can be put on dogs bed as a flea deterrent. Great for animals in their food supply

Nutritional values; As well as B and C vitamins it also contains Magnesium, Potassium, Iron, Phosphorous and Calcium.

What is really exciting about Herb Robert is its levels of Germanium which are in a lot of plants but more so in the Geranium family and most noted in Herb Robert.

Germanium allows O2 to be carried around the body by causing electrical impulses (you may also like to read 'The Invisible Rainbow') to connect at a cellular level. We are after all electrical beings! **One of the prime growth of cancer cells can be attributed to lack of Oxygen. Cancer cannot exist in the presence of Oxygen. (Other factors that increase cancer cells are acidic** *environments, dairy products, excess sugar which creates acidity.)* Dr Ottor Warburg: *cancer cannot exist in presence of abundant O2 environments.*

Isabella Shipard studies show Herb Robert as a healer for Cancer, Colitis, Chronic Fatigue, Cataracts, Diabetes, mouth ulcers, Arthritis and chemical poisoning.

For radiation poisoning or detox Julia recommends seeping a handful in 1 litre of water and drinking daily.

Herb Robert can increases energy in the body and has antiviral and antioxidant properties, removes toxins and builds immunity. Helps reduce radiation into the body from the effects of EMRs such as 5G.

Double check if you are on blood thinners.

(Another favourite of Julia's is Speedwell; Named because of the Speed it spread from the introduction of transport increasing, or as Julia says the speed it heals, depending on which theory you follow!

Above Just starting to flower in April Herb Robert (Helston passage.) It will go red/purple as the summer develops and then becomes easier to identify.

Above; Wild Chervil (Wild Carrot) similar to Hemlock, compared to leaves on Herb Robert (Right) which form in a circular or star pattern at the end of the stem rather than off the stem in a feathery pattern. We refer to these leave shapes as Lace like hence 'Queen's Anne's Lace, 'Wild Carrot,' Daucus carota distinguishes itself from Hemlock with small pink flowers usually in the centre of it's beautiful array of white flowers. ALWAYS TRACE THE STEM OF HERB ROBERT IT CAN GROW AMONGST HEMLOCK AND PICK WHEN ITS PINK FLOWERS ARE OUT TO BE ABSOLUTELY SURE!

Hogweed, (*Heracleum spondyliu***), Common Hogweed.**

Umbellifer family.

Its Story; Also named Cow Parsnip. Not to be confused with **Giant Hogweed** that has **purple blotches** on the stems and a more tropical shape leaf standing 10 to 12 ft compared to 6ft of Hogweed. I personally have not seen any Giant Hogweed in Cornwall as yet?

Hogweed does not have the lace like leaf patterns that Hemlock has.

As an Umbellifer it is cousin of the carrot and can reach up to 6ft. **Hairy not scary stems.(*)** Giant Hogweed has fairly smooth stems with tiny white hairs and usually purple blotches.

According to **Messegue** (the great French herbalist) as a child he would dry the stems out and a sugary edible substance would ooze out. However do not expose the sap to sun if it is on your skin and on the whole do not eat the leaves and stem raw they are better cooked.

Everyday food; Despites some infamous stories about this plant, Common Hogweed is a favourite with some Foragers. The new shoots can be fried in tapioca batter and are simply delicious and the unopened flower buds are also delicious steamed. It is Roger Philip's favourite food, he compares it to Asparagus.

Use the seeds like Cardamom they are like green peppercorns and black are like black peppercorns. The seeds and seed shells are becoming more popular. (see Galloway Wild Foods who have experimented with sweet and savoury delights.) It is an acquired taste; spicy but earthy at the same time!

Medicinally; Messegue refers to its past name *Heracleum* as it was dedicated to *Hercules* because it was a powerful plant and great tonic.. he used leaves and roots for boils, ulcers, abscesses and insect bites.

Swedes (not the veg the people!) love this plant and claim it can treat *Hysteria and Epilepsy,* The Russians use the root for serious digestive upsets such as *Dysentry*.

Messegue's Father used it as an aphrodisiac; *'Many an impotent man and a frigid woman has been restored to..normal sexual functioning.'* Delivered through footbaths of leaves and roots or teaspoons daily from the juice.

Astonishingly it has more protein, Magnesium and Phosphorus than Nettles which are normally hard to beat in most areas. See table below.

Plant	Water (%)	Potassium (mg/100g)	Phosphorous (mg/100g)	Magnesium (mg/100g)	Calcium (mg/100g)	Iron (mg/100g)
Curly Kale (cultvtd)	86.3	490	87	31	212	1.9
Stinging Nettle	84.8	410	105	71	630	7.8
Common Hogweed	79.8	540	125	75	320	3.2

Above; Common Hogweed another undervalued plant; see the nutritional comparison.

Mallow, (*Malva sylvestri.*)

Its Story There are many types of Mallow, 'sylvestris, or Common Mallow is often called *'The last plant In England,'* because of its proximity to the sea, It is the first plant you will see on this walk and I find it quite magical, it looks like a furry little bush or tree with soft pink and dark maroon flowers.

Juliette Levy (Julia Of The Herbs) suggested all Mallows should be allowed to grow where they occur because of their immense value to herbalists.

Valued as a food for centuries and linked to love potions in Mythology.

Also known as the *'mortification plant'* because of its high mucilage content, it was used to preserve bodies.

Its seed or 'cheeses' as they were known as they look like cheese wheels, were regularly chewed and eaten by children. What a healthy snack!

Its tough branches have also been used as a form of cloth or fibre and a business was established here in West Cornwall with the trade name **'Brotex**,' to develop this, which unfortunately folded.

It goes without saying, when you look at those stunning flowers that it is loved by the bees and it grows up to 8ft tall.

Everyday Use; All the plant is edible, you can put the flowers in your salad, stir fry, or make a lovely tea with them.

The stems are tasty and leaves which can also be eaten raw as the hairs are softer than Cleavers; so not as irritating, but always test them first as older leaves can be rougher. Its mucilage has been used as a thickener

Medicinally; The mucus has been used as an artificial saliva for cancer patients.

The Mucilage or 'sweet muscilin' as Ray called it has immense healing powers and can be used as a soother a bit like Aloe Vera. You can also find some mucilage in the stalks and leaves.

It is full of vitamins A, B and C, Omega 3 and 6, protein, antioxidants, Iron, Potassium and Calcium, it can also protect the liver.

Despite being a gentle soothing plant it is a powerful *expectorant*, meaning it can get rid of mucus. It is an anti inflammatory and a repairer

Above; The beautiful Mallow flower at Godrevy; all the plant is edible.

Mullein, *Verbascum spp.*

Its Story; Big fluffy leaves and yellow flower spikes. This beautiful medicinal plant is really easy to identify. It is Biennial.

It has a long association with **Witches and healing.**

Leave hairs can be irritating hence its name 'Quaker rouge' from the Quaker girls who would rub on their cheeks to make their cheeks red like rouge.

Used as a broth for cattle to rid coughs and a poultice for injured horses hooves.

Everyday Food; I just dry these leaves out and make tea with nettle for a winter tonic.

Medicinally; Calms and strengthens the nervous and urinary system.

Great for swollen glands and respiratory issues. Has been used to treat Pleurisy and Pneumonia as an antibiotic replacement. Its furry leaves can be smoked. It has Expectorant (breaks up Mucus) and has antiseptic actions.

A powerful pain reliever and de wormer. Make a tincture with the root.

Mullein will also draw out splinters and boils.

Mullein flower oil is a **natural remedy for earache** and Julie Bruton-Seale (Hedgerow Healing) swears by it. (see recipe at the end.)

Used for Plantar fasciitis by putting the leaves in your shoe and change regularly. It is also anti fungal so will clear up Athletes Foot.

Pick leaves just before flowering; they are easy to dry in the sun. Keep a jar to make tea with or smoke the leaves for winter colds.

Leaves and flowers are known to relieve stubborn coughs (also see Plantain.)

Helps spinal issues and setting bones (as does Comfrey and Daisy.)

Julie Bruton- Seale's ear remedy for her son pour olive oil over dried Mullein flowers and seal with with a cloth . Leave in a sunny place for two weeks and stir each day. Sieve into another jar and then a third jar leaving the watery substance. Use 1 to 3 drops in ears. Can be stored in darkness for a year.

Above; The beautiful big fluffy leaves and sun yellow flowers of Mullein are a delight to some and are prolific around the Cornish coast.

Nettle (*Uritica dioica.***)**

Its Story; Nettles were one of the sacred herb of Anglo Saxons and so it should be!

A very revered plant in past times and In Denmark a chieftan was discovered wrapped in Nettle fibre around 2800 years ago.

Nettles is undoubtedly one of the best plants for health. **Hippocrates himself wrote 61 different nettle based remedies!**

Ancient records show a Sage known as Milarepa (1052 – 1135) was supposed to live off Nettle soup!

As a warming and stimulating plant the Scottish have used Nettles to whip themselves before a cold water swim to increase circulation so they didn't get too cold.

Maria Treben (Health From God's Garden), describes Nettle as growing in areas of natural Electro Magnetic Fields and she says the fibrous stem has been used (and still is it's making a comeback) to make clothing.

Everyday food; I chop the tops of Nettles off before they have seeded and collect a couple of buckets full I then steam them slightly and roll them into a ball and freeze for soup and stews in winter. Once seeded do not collect the leaves as they contain Calcium Carbonate crystals which can irritate the Kidneys; collect the **heavy female seeds** and dry them out fully then put through a sieve, before storing them in a jar for energy , vitality and an adrenal tonic..they are natures 'Speed' **they give a healthy energy boost. .. The Romans and Greeks used these seeds as an aphrodisiac.**

Also juice nettles with apple and Grass for a super immunity boost; a masticator juicer works best.

You can make a cake with Nettles as The '**Knowledge To Forage**,' crew have in their amazing book.

Medicinally; Nettles are high in most vitamins particularly C, the **leaves** are rich in minerals, Chlorophyll, Lecithin, Cartenoids, Flavonoids, Sterols, Tannin, and Iron. **Nettles are natural histamines mean they can alleviate allergies and Hay Fever.**

Whipping parts of the body with nettles forces the body to produce Nitric Acid a vasodilator meaning it widens the blood vessels helping blood to flow better. This can be used for High Blood Pressure.

Nettles Increase immunity, reduces blood sugar so great for Diabetes ,Collic and Gout.

Nettles have seven neuro transmitters inside each tiny hair on its stem including serotonin so Nettle soup or Nettle juice with apple two to three times a week can keep depression and anxiety at bay. Nettle **Hairs'** also contain Formic Acid, Choline and Histamine..

Artemis Simopoulos discovered that Omega 3s which are so lacking in the modern diet can be extracted in large numbers from plants; no greater examples is The Nettle.

Nettles are high in antioxidants will seek out and neutralise unnatural free radicals which try to mimic and imitate natural hormones a great problem with modern food known as **EDCs; Endocrine Disrupting Chemicals (see Theo Coleburn.)**

Above; Some of the known benefits of the rejuvenating Nettle plant.

Above; Seb collecting Nettles by Snipping the top 10 to 15cm off. Remember don't pick <u>once they have flowered.</u>

Pennywort (*Centella asiatica),Ubbilicus.* Naval Wort, Wall Pennywort, Gotu Kola.

Its Story; Umbilicus *refers to the belly button in the middle of the leaf,* hence 'Centella Asiatica.' Gotu Kola.

Native to Britain, Europe and North Africa but loved in Asia and used globally. **Think of it as a British Aloe Vera a succulent with similar healing and cooling effects.**

Grows from rocks and walls and can taste different depending on where it grows from.

King Aruna in 10th century used Pennywort to boost his energy and stamina.

Popular in Ayurvedic medicine and in the East they say in English; *'A **Pennywort a day keeps old age away.'** Chinese medicine calls it 'Source Of Life' as it secures longlife after herbalist* **Li Ching Yeun** *was said to live to 256 and drank Pennywort tea most of his life amongst other plants.*

Russ Maslen wrote a book about freeing his wife Beryl from Arthritis with the use of Pennywort.(Moolihai.com.)

Everyday food; Eat raw from the hedge in salads like a cucumber or mange tout. Fry up in a stir fry.

Medicinally; Contains high levels of Omega 3s and Vitamin E.as well as Vitamin B, C,K , Manganese, Potassium, Phosphorous and Zinc.

Penywort have a lot of anti-inflammatory, and antiseptic qualities used for Diabetes and depression. Can inhibit bacterial growth and contains flavonoids rich in antioxidants.

Cooling for all organs and has a diuretic effect ..a plant very much valued by Culpeper who described it as **'Kidneywort' because its helps to heal kidneys 'torn or fretted by the stone.'**

Can boost memory, heal skin, improve cardiovascular and brain health..

Small studies recently have shown to reduce **Alzheimer's disease.**

Studies in 2000 showed a significant reduction in **Depression and Anxiety** and panic attack disorders on a controlled group using Pennywort extract daily.

Pennywort above, often seen growing off trees or walls and can vary from the size of a 50p coin to the size of a large plate.

Pineapple Weed (*Matricaria discoidea.***)**

Its Story; Flower look like Daisy or Camomile without its petals and its feathery leaves smell of pineapple. It is closely related to Camomile and Mayweed . All are edible.

Contains an aromatic oil which is used in the perfume industry.

Indigenous people at Cheyenne Sundance Ceremonies burned Pineapple Weed with the hair of a loved one to prevent them from leaving them.

Everyday food; Use in jelly and syrups, dry and use like Camomile tea, pop leaves and flowers into salads.

Medicinally; Word of mouth from Native Americans suggest that Pineapple Weed has been used for treating colds, *flu, fevers as a de wormer or parasite cleanser, for stomach complaints and menstrual cramps.*

It has Analgesic properties so relieves pain and can protect wounds from infection and help heal quicker. It can also be used as an insect repellent.

Above Pineapple Weed can be quite low to the ground ranging from 5cm to 30cm.

Plantain. *Plantago coronopus;* **Buckhorn Plantain,** *Plantago major ;* **Broadleaf Plantain** *,Plantago lanceolata;* **Ribwort Plantain.**

There is a Sea Plantain too (Maritima) which I have never seen.

Its Story; Originally from Europe but known in America as **'White Man's Foot,'** as the tiny seeds attached to travellers feet and spread to America where the Native Americans used it to make a super popular ointment or balm for soothing bites and wounds.

Plantain is one of the nine ancient herbs of The Saxons.

Everyday food; We roll our Plantain leaves with common Sorrel to make two contrasting taste alkaline and acid ..yum! Put the leaves in salads.

The seeds are rich in Vitamin B and can be fried with butter or oil to make into crisps taste 'mushroomy' delights.

Medicinally; Plantain is the real Dock leaf and soother, taking Nettle stings out in 30 seconds, Bee stings in 3 minutes, and used for many angry skin conditions such as Eczema, Acne and Psoriasis.

Plantain will draw pus and venom out of wounds.

To extract the Plantain juice, roll the leaf up and put pressure on the heal of hand till the green juice squeezes out. This will take histamine out very quickly.

To create Plantain balm; *collect a basket full of leaves, squeeze juice out into pan up to an inch high put in a glug of Olive oil or coconut oil heat gently and put through a sieve then in the fridge to create a green balm.*

Goes with Yarrow and Slippery Elm as a soothing cleansing poultice.

Internally Use as a mouthwash for swollen gums, *'As within so without ,'* Plantain is very alkalizing and has been used for stomach ulcers, irritable bowl as it soothes mucus membranes; the leaves can stop bleeding so good for Ulcerative Colitis.

Ribwort (which has obvious ribs up and down the leaf,) is known to treat coughs particularly stubborn bronchial coughs and will earth up stubborn mucus.

Broadleaf can be put in shoes to treat plantar fasciitis and Native Americans put them in their shoes to ease tired feet.

Seed heads; Are full of Omega 3, oil, protein and fibre..similar to Flaxseeds. Nutty fibrous, protein can be soaked like Chia seeds. Can ease constipation.

Above Ribwort Plantain having seeded. You cannot fail to identify the ribs on the leaves of this beautiful soothing plants.

Rock Samphire (*Critmum maritimum.*)

Its Story; From the French name for St Peter (St Pierre) who is patron saint of the sea, also in it family is Sea Pickle, Sea Bean, Sea Asparagus.

It is protected so only take small amounts. Found on cliff faces, succulent Reindeer horns and yellow/white flowers (Spring to Autumn.)

As a *Halophyte* a plant that grows in areas of high salinity, is high in sodium which contains an array of minerals.

Everyday food; Eat both leaf and flowers but the 'perfumey' taste gets milder once cooked. Leaves can be fried or pickled to go with cheese.

Medicinally; Samphire is rich in vitamins and minerals particularly vitamin A an C. It is also a rich source of **Magnesium** which can affect hormones and moods if we do not take enough of.

It is full of anti oxidants due to it containing **Fucoidans** which sea vegetables contain and is a good anti inflammatory and is a great digestive aid.

Above; Rock Samphire. If you want Magnesium in your diet this is the plant!

Rose Bay Willow Herb (*Chamerion angustifolium.*)

Its Story; So so pretty this one, often see it amongst the evening primrose (of which it is part of this family) with a stunning display of pink flowers that form a non uniformed foxglove shape.

Its seeds fill the air like fairies.

Often grows on land that has had fires ..like a Phoenix.which explains one of its other names *Fireweed and Bombweed after WW2.*

Leaves have veins which reach out to the edge but return back to the centre. Hard to identify as a young shoot but delicious if you are confident.

Flowers and leaves can be eaten and the fermented leaves are used to make a delicious drink called **Ivan Chai** which is supposed to extend human life. **Hitler thought Ivan Chai gave The Red Army its strength so much so that he bombed and destroyed some of the factories making it.**

Everyday food; Make Ivan Chai..see above and recipe at the end, or simply put the flowers and leaves into salads.

Medicinally; Rich in C and A studies show it high in Polyphenols, Cartenoids, Antioxidants and Flavonoids.

Used medicinally for skin issues. The raw stem can also draw pus out and prevent a cut form healing too quickly

Used for upset stomachs particularly from undercooked meals. Generally calms and can be treated for stomach ulcers too

In Europe tinctures can be bought from this plant to help with urinary and prostrate problems and some studies have used Rose Bay Willow Herb for **Prostate Cancer.**

How to make Ivan Cha in four easy steps;

1. Collect leaves and leave them to wilt for 24 hours in a dark place.

2. Next day rub the leaves to bruise them and place them in a ceramic dish place a tea towel over the top and leave for a further 24 hours in a warm dark place.

3. Day 3; Put on a very low oven with the door open, turning the leaves until they are dry and then leave again overnight

4. Crumble them into a jar and make a tea using one teaspoon at **time.**

Above Rosebay Willow Herb a beautiful pink/ purple display in the hedge.

Sea Beet (Beta Vulgaris Maritima), Sea Spinach.

Its Story; Wild ancestor to beetroot, swish chard and spinach.

Belongs to one of many subspecies of the Beet family known as the Pigweed family or previously Goose Foot family.

Mabey recommends to pick between April and October

Ancient food and medicine. **Found in Mesolithic and Neolithic sites and archelogical sites in Egypt.**

Origin may have come from the Middle East spread along Atlantic sea to the Mediterranean.

Gathered and sold in Ireland today.

Everyday Food; In the Isle of Wight it is gathered to eat alongside pork or bacon. It is popular all around Europe including Spain and Portugal. France mixes it with Sorrel to balance the bitter taste..Russia use it as a base for soup and the roots were ground and mixed with flour during famine. Many old recipes use it with beans and lentils.

I use Sea Beet like Spinach generally cooking it in curries, Risotto, stir fries or a layer in a lasagne. The raw taste is quite bitter but you rarely notice it once cooked

Medicinally; High Vitamn C, K, B and A, Calcium Zinc, iron. High in dietary fibre.

There are a lot of remedies for cultivated beets, particularly using the roots, but Greek physician Galen wrote that Wild Beet was more effective than cultivated varieties. In general wild plants have been identified in modern studies (see Royal School Of Pharmacy 2006) to be significantly more nutritious than cultivated varieties.

References say leaves were chewed for Glaucoma, a poultice on the foot for sciatica, on the wrist for scabies and the juice for wolf wounds!

As far back as 100bc has been referred to relieve headaches, ear pain, dandruff, soothing chillblains, shin sores and treating leprosy.

References in 16th century (Jean Ruel) refer to treating Colic.

Records show a decoction can be prepared to treat Leukaemia, Breast and Womb cancers as well as stomach head and spleen issue with Sea Beet (liber Canonis Medicine 1845).

Most of the Beet family refer to healing of the liver ..Hepatitis, Jaundice and fatty liver plus Aneameia , bruises, burns, inflammation, gas, digestive complaints , fever and various cancers.

Juice is a catalyst for Oxygen and so prevents tumour growth..whilst high in iron and Silic acid which regenerates red blood cells. Sea Beet is both Anti oxidant and Anti inflammatory.

Roots and leaves remedy for fatty liver, Hepatitis, Anaemia and in South Africa decoction of the leaves for Haemorrhoids.

Should be avoided by people with renal or kidney issues due to high levels of Oxalates.

Left; a drawing of Sea Beet from my notebook.

Above;Clusters of Sea Beet grow abundantly in specific areas around Cornwall; Gwithian, Polzeath, Porthtowan to name a few.

Sea Buckthorn, *Hippophae rhamnoides (Sandthorn, Sallowthorn, Seaberry.)*

It Story; Well my goodness, Ray could not stop talking about this plant he grew the tree version in his forest garden from the Himalayas but the bush version *Hippophae rhamnoides* is native to North Europe and the Southern tip of the UK including Cornwall.

One of its names was **Wonder Plant** for reasons you are about to understand.

Recent developers tore it out of a building development in Hayle saying it was an invasive foreign plant. They couldn't be further from the truth; not only does it stabilise the sand it has one of the most nutritious bright orange berries in the world! Ray provided me with the information for my banner at a local protest for people who really have only an interest in money and fail to investigate the plants and their value in the area. It is Native to Southern Britainn and Northern Europe!

From modern Greek word 'Hippo' meaning horse and Phaos means shine as it was said to give shine to horses following its alleged healing properties to 'give light' or cure horses of blindness. It could also refer to the shiny silvery part of the under part of the leaf. Leaves and young branches allowed horsed to gain weight and produce a super shiny coat.

Alexander The Great, not only fed it to his horses but berries to his soldiers which was said to win him his final battles. Plants have been known to win wars (see Rosebay Willow Herb and Yarrow)

An ancient plant used for healing all over the world particularly in Tibet. The nutritional value of this plant were recorded in the 8th century Tibet (see Li and Guo 1989) In Russia it is referred to as 'Siberian Pineapple' because of its taste and juiciness.

Russians then investigated it for its properties in fruit, leaves and bark. It was used in this country as a protection (like Herb Robert) against radiation. Unfortunately the UK continue to deny that EMFs and EMR is harmful which leaves us on a back foot for health.

The Chinese have been propagating this plant for centuries and establishing plantations particularly since the 1980s where they have used it in sports drinks to help their Athletes in the Olympics; no wonder they did so well!

Many Beetles Aphids and Moths rely on this plant.

Everyday food; Leaves can be dried for tea and its berries have one of the **highest contents of Vitamin C (780mg/100mg).**

To get the berries cut a few branches off and freeze them. Once frozen shake off the berries. Pop them in desserts, smoothies, salads or even a Gin and Tonic!

Medicinally; Sea Buckthorn has many bioactive ingredients that would normally require several plants to get the high level of nutrients that Sea Buckthorn provides; it can stop coughs and is great for pain relief, fever, inflammation, abscesses, tumours and constipation.

It has 200 nutritional and bioactive compounds..it is anti many things; anti –cancer, anti-obesity, anti-viral..the list goes on and is loaded with fatty acids responsible for vitamin transportation from cell to cell.

A summary would say the Vitamin C content of this plant is off the scale it has an absolute array of mineral contents (I.e Manganese, Phosphorus, Iron, Boron etc) What is really fascinating is its 2 to 8 % fat content which disperses a high Vitamin E content and bioactive compound; it is an absolute superfood and when you see its berries please pick and eat them with joy and respect for the healing this plant can offer you! Seriously **if you were stranded on a Desert Island and this plant showed up, thank your lucky stars it is a saviour and Ray knew that..that is why he grew it.**

Sea Buckthorn

Found near The Bluff in Hayle and Hervey Towans. Also quite abundant around North Devon; Saunton Sands particularly.

Sea Cabbage, (*Brassica olerace.*)

Different from Sea Kale (Crambe Maritima) we think, but information can be confusing. Sea Kale is more rare around Cornwall and has purple flowers but they all from the ***Cruciferae family referring to the cross of Jesus because their flowers have four petals.***

Not only is it more flavoursome than garden cabbage but studies have shown it is less prone to pests. It gets it toughness from the sea and will be full of minerals, like all coastal foraged food it gets nutrients from the sea air and the rain storms that feed it with a vast array of minerals.

Wild Sea Cabbage has beautiful yellow flowers like the Wild Radish and Wild Mustard you will see.

Everyday food; As well as steaming with a roast and a tad of butter, I also crisp up with butter or coconut oil in the oven with Halloumi and chilli.

Medicinally; Sea Cabbage are also rich in Folate, Vitamin K, Vitamin A and C Also full of Phytonutrients, so they are great for decreasing inflammation.

Above; Sea Cabbage in my garden note the yellow cruciferous petals and beautiful pale green leaves with a blue tinge..take your supermarket cabbage and times this by 10 for nutrition and taste.

Above; a Sea Cabbage, Three Cornered Leek and mushroom risotto. On the side, their flowers over cucumber, artichoke and vine leaves.

Sea Campion *(Silena uniflora)*

Unmistakeable when in Flower and one of my favourites. Leaves are salty and the flower has a really interesting sharp but sweet taste. One Forager described the taste as 'pleasingly metallic.' Either way it is a great experience.

Nectar rich and invaluable to wildlife.

Similar to Bladder Campion which is also edible.

Everyday food; Unless cooking don't eat in huge quantities as contains Saponins (found in beans) which are poisonous but are not absorbed well in the human body so pass through the system, however best to use the leaves sparingly in salads. Flowers are fine.

Medicinally; Campions **(of any species)** were used to **treat internal bleeding, kidney disease, sores and ulcers, and stings.** Healers also used it to treat warts and corns. In Spain and Italy, the plant was used for digestive disorders

Above Sea Campion has a really aromatic taste, just a few are perfect in a salad with its little salty leaves and aromatic flower. Best used in small amounts due to its high Saponin content.

Sea Holly *(Eryngo varifolium).*

Its Story; Flowers intense blue. Silver/grey leaves with blue veins.

Flowers become egg shaped and are edible and slightly aromatic

Root is edible and taste like chestnuts. Used to be coated in sugar and sold as as sweet known as 'Kissing comforts' because of their aphrodisiac qualities. (originally made popular by Colchester Apothecary)

Used around trees as a protection from vermin.

Everyday food; Root used to be dried and mixed with sugar as a sweet, they can also be sliced and used in salad. New leaves can also be eaten.

Medicinally; Root known to to improve '**loss of vital force,'** in older people.

Used to treat liver, chest and glandular disorders as well as constipation and The Arabs cook new roots for deficiency of minerals particularly Silica.

Above; The Bees love the beautiful ethereal Sea Holly like this one buzzing (Low left) at Godrevy

Sea Radish (*Raphanus maritime***)**

Its Story; According to Juliette Levy, Sea Radish is quite rare so we have plenty of it dotted around Cornwall particularly on this stretch of coast. It is very peppery and powerful in taste.

Everyday food; Use sparingly in salads or a curry.

Medicinally: With 'pungent root' the Sea Radish is a great tonic for the blood, Gout, constipation as well as bladder and kidney disorders.

A great detox plant with anti inflammatory properties and high in Vitamin C

Above;This beautiful sample of Sea Radish was found on The Helford river but you can identify them fully when they flower; as part of the Cruciferous family they have similar yellow four petal flowers.

Sorrel (*Rumex Acetosa.*)Cuckoo's Meat.

Its Story; Many different types..from French *Surele* from **Sur meaning sour.**

Culpepper refers to this plant as under the domain of Venus ..Goddess Of Love and has been used since Grecian times.

Used with eggs..by Queen Anne, Charles 2nd and James 2nd amongst others..used in omelettes and egg tarts.

Mashed with salt and sugar to make 'Green Sauce' common with fish, Pork or goose.

Wartime children used to suck the leaves to help with spots.

Doesn't dry well so best frozen if you want to store it.

John Evelyn loved sorrel and proclaimed no salad is complete without it!

Everyday food; Addition to salads and can use like spinach.

Medicinally; cooling, diuretic, anti inflammatory, purifies, detoxes, laxative, **kills intestinal worms** , used for **Fevers, Jaundice, tumours, skin disease, ulcerated bowl and kidney disease**.

Root and Seed is an astringent ..great for Haemorrhages and as a blood purifier.

Historically has been mixed with Thistle tops and Dandelion to treat Consumption.

High Vitamin C means it has been used a cure for Scurvy in the Isle of Man, Orkney, Shetlands and Faeroe Islands. In dact Sorrel has **More Vitamin C in one leaf than an orange.**

Good Calcium content so good for anti ageing.

Oxalic Acid; Excess Oxalic Acid can produce crystals so should not be consumed in high amounts as it may irritate any liver and kidney disease rather than help. However Katrina Blair reports that Oxalic acid tones the Colon and encourages Peristalsis and elimination and tends to think that the excess crystalizaton found in kidneys and liver can result from excess meat, processed foods and acidic beverages...remember ECDs Endocrine Disruptive Chemicals (see Theo Coleburn.) Most Antioxidants contain high levels of Oxalic acid

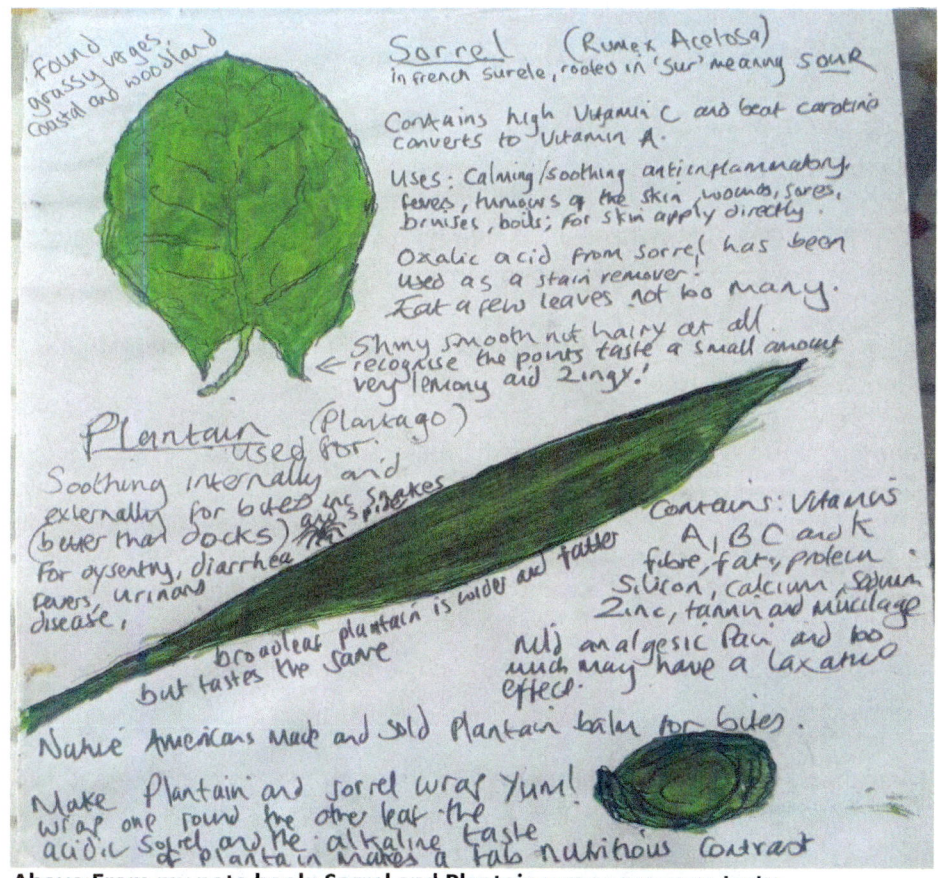

Above;From my note book; Sorrel and Plantain wraps are very tasty.

Sowthistle (*Sonchus spp*)

Its Story; Introduced by The Romans used as a winter veg.

Hollow stem distinguishes it from Wild Lettuce although it looks similar. (Wild Lettuce is less common and has a solid dtem not a hollow stem, but is great for pain relief known as **'Nature's Diazepam.'**)

The Sow part is because it was said to increase Sow's milk.

Part of the Dandelion family but has a more refreshing taste and produces multiple flowers on one stem. **One of my favourites.**

Other names include Hare Thistle for the hares fondness of the weed it was said to 'hide the hare and keep it from its melancholy!'(J. Levy)

Some great fans of Sowthistle including John Kallas who compares the juicy stems as 'Sowsparagus'..flavour like Asparagus or Artichoke heart.

Galen talks about the Moroccan Ambassador who enjoyed it in a salad as honoured as a wild delight.

Maoris made a chewing gum from the milky sap and its feathery seeds have been used to stuff pillows.

Everyday food; Use this amazing leaf in salad or munch on it whilst walking for hydration.

The tap root can be eaten like Potato and like Dandelion can be used as a Coffee substitute;

Medicinally; Polyphenolic content is four times more than red wine and 12 times more than black tea. Kallas also claims it is rich in fatty acids, Zinc, **Manganese, Copper, Iron, Calcium and fibre high in ABC and K per 100g**

has 30 to 60 mg of Vitamin C and smooth varieties have 800mg of Vitamin A.

Similar qualities to Dandelion good for detoxing liver and kidney. The leaves are used in parts of Italy for their diuretic and laxative qualities.

Above; A beautiful example of Sow Thistle in April along the Helford passage note the leaves on this one do not have little prickles. They do vary. The leaves are slightly lighter than Dandelion but you will recognise the flower buds as part of this family. Background we see Herb Robert, Hedge Bedstraw and Cleavers.

Thistles *(C.Vulgare) Spear Thistle.*

There are 14 types of Thistle in the UK today you will probably see The Spear Thistle in this area.

Its Story; Despite the Thistle being on the noxious weed list it has been the Scottish national symbol since the 1200s. **Legend has it that one of the Viking invaders sneaking upon a Scottish camp trod upon a thistle and cried out in pain alerting the Scottish to the danger.**

It is the Celtic symbol for nobility and strength.

In Norse mythology the Thistle was considered to be the **lightening plant** and Thor the god of thunder would protect anyone who used or wore the Thistle.

Thistles take care of the land, they will only hold dominance of the land early on, they provide a rainbow of nutrients to the top soil and they break up soil compaction and aerate the soil to allow life forms like Earthworms in.

Interestingly, plants that have spikes for protection do not tend to be bitter as the spikes cover their protection.

Everyday food; All thistles are edible. According to Katrina Blair all Thistle flowers can be chewed; below the beautiful purple colour is a light fluff which can be used as chewing gum and they help clean your teeth.

Seeds can be made into a nutritious milk blended with honey and vanilla.

The spiky leaves can be juiced as a real tonic for the liver.

The stalk is like a sweet celery and contains mineralized water and is highly alkaline.

Medicinally; Thistle reminds me of Burdock; its leaves and roots are great for the liver.

Katrina Blair loves **The Thistle and explains that its alkaline effect on the body can give a natural high unlike marijuana and psychedelic drugs that provide a high through an alkaloid** which then returns to acid once the high is gone. **The 'high' obtained from Thistle is long term with no withdrawal.**

Permaculture.co.uk describes a Portuguese study where they sold the mid rib of thistle at markets and on tests comparing with the market vegetables; *'Weight for weight, thistles came out higher in fibre, protein, Phosphorus, Magnesium, Calcium, Copper, Zinc and other nutrients.'*

So Thistle is really underrated!

Above; An underestimated treasure; Spear Thistle a common sight on the dunes.

Three Cornered leek (*Allium Triquetrium.)*

left the triangular shape of the Three Cornered Leek on the right compared to the Bluebell on the left; they are often picked by mistake and the Bluebell is toxic. Observe the shape and smell the leaf to be sure of your identification.

Its Story; Named because of the stem with three markers forming a triangle shape.

Green stripe white bell flowers .Can be mistaken for white Bluebell species.

Cultivated since 1759 according to Miles Irving.

Milder than Ramson (Wild Garlic) that tends to grow in acid soil in woodlands.

In 1955 you could be fined for allowing it to grow as it is so invasive.

Found mostly in the South west coastal areas, Isles, some in London.

Spreads rapidly **so picking large quantities is not seen as an issue.**

Everyday food; Use leaves and flowers as spring onions so great in salads, Quiche or make Wild Leek Pesto. In spring you will not need to buy onions hurray!!

Medicinally; Digestive, blood aid, reduces cholesterol, great for circulation and has antioxidants, vitamins and minerals.

Above; Hey it's spring; forget buying onions and spring onion;ThreeCornered Leeks are super abundant..here's a Friday night in April and it is frying mushrooms in butter and garlic add cream then throw in this sea cabbage with it's beautiful Cruciferous (cross; 4 petalled flowers) and the Three Cornered Leek then add rice, stock and water; a tasty risotto.

Yarrow (Achillea millefolium)

Its Story; Umbelifer shaped pretty flowers BUT **from the Daisy family not the Umbelifers.**

Names after Achilles the warrior who was thought to use the plant to staunch the wound of his fellow soldiers, winning him the battle, however he was not so lucky! **Achille's Mother was supposed to dip him into a magical river so he would have eternal life. Other stories suggest it was a barrel of Yarrow tea he was held upside down and so protected. The arrow that shot into his heal bone was not covered with this magical tea as he was held by his ankle when dipped and so he died of his injury hence the term 'Achilles Heal,' or weak spot!**

According to Erin Verinder in her book 'Plants For The People' **Yarrow is 'master of the blood'** with the capacity to cease blood flow. It is also adaptive and balancing and can encourage blood flow. The SAS are taught to use Yarrow. It truly is a wonderful plant!

In many herbal books they talk of an Ale that used to be made from Yarrow which had relaxing and possible mind altering affects!

Everyday food; Make a lovely tea with fresh or dried leaves and flowers. Put in salads but sparingly as it has a strong taste. Tea helps with sleep.

Medicinally; Yarrow is an essential part of a First Aid kit. Put up nostrils to lessen nose bleeds and directly onto wounds to clean and stop blood flow., also used to stop uterine bleeding in a bath after childbirth.

It has **antiseptic** actions so will stop infection on the wound as well.

Whilst stopping bleeding it can also encourage bleeding and circulation so is great for the heart. **It adapts to the situation needed; Clever plant!**

Yarrow encourages sweat but can also help break a Fever (Diaphoretic.)

It is a great plant for the skin and the Native Americans often used it for digestive issues. As a cousin of Camomile it has calming effects and can be used for pets in this way. Amongst peasant communities used a Quinine but also its anti proliferative actions (stopping cellular growth) making it of huge interest for cancer treatments and research.

The root is rarely used but can be applied to gums to ease toothache, however Nicky Allen one of the Uk's most famous Psychic Mediums, recently went to the 'Angel realm'in one of her transformational journeys and was offered Yarrow Root to heal her ME; she was told the name of the plant and had no idea it existed and looked it up to find it has been used for auto immune conditions such as ME, MS and Fibromyalgia.

Above; Yarrow: A stunning medicinal plants; the white variety is usually the one found in the wild Achillea Millefollium. The roots is also beneficial.

Additional plants of interest you find more in land.

Self Heal *(Prunella Vulgaris) Heal All, Carpenters Herb, Heart of The Earth*

Its Story; *Same family as mint and like all this family has a square stem and has beautiful shades of purple flowers. Bees love it.*

Ancient people saw this flower as open mouths with little tongues which links to its healing properties in the mouth and throat. When we come more sensitive to plants features they often can look similar to their healing qualities like the Walnut looks like a little brain and is good for the brain. These observations are often talked about in tribes and' sensory herbalism,' circles and this plant's name should draw your attention to its qualities!

Everyday food; *Use flower and leaves in salads.*

Medicinally; *Rich in vitamin A, B, C and K as well as Flavanoids.* **Self Heal is an anti-inflammatory, anti-oxidant, stimulates lymphatic system, treats heart disease, tumours and infections such as sore throat and mouth ulcers**.

Research shows that compounds in this amazing plant can kill cancerous cells and inhibits enzymes that can promote cancer cells.

Above; Self Heal a small flower on grassland and dunes a bit larger than Red Clover with many healing benefits.

Herb Bennett Geum urbanum (*Wood Averns.*)

Same family as Burdock. **Geum** mening agreeable fragrance and **Urbanum** as it was found in the city.

Everyday Food; Use the root ground in a vinegarette or to flavour stews or apple crumbles to add some spice.

Medicinal; Roots same medicinal qualities as Cloves they are spicy and smell good can be used for toothache and digestive orders.

Abov; Herb Bennett /Wood Averns, When I was into 'neat gardening,' I pulled this out many times..what a mistake it's a beautiful plants and its root is very powerful.

Lady's Mantle *(Alchemilla Vulgaris) Roseaceae*

Its Story; This plant really interests me as a woman in her 50s along with red *Clover and Dandelion for Menopause*. In Arabic referred to as *Alkemelych* from the word **Alchemists** which proves the high esteem for this plant.

Leaves were considered to look like the mantles worn by ladies. It seems to regulate hormonal imbalances in women but was originally used to heal wounds. A German gynaecologist claimed that taking Lady's mantle over a long period of time would have *'spared many Gynaecological operations.'*(Loewenfeld.)

Everyday Food; Fresh leaves with salads and make a powerful tea with the flowers.

Medicinally; Used to restore normal menstruation for women and ease inflamed fertility organs. **Women from 40 upwards were advised to drink a tea of it 10 days a month to ease 'the change.' Other healing qualities include, heart, sluggish blood, weak arteries and Diabetes.**

Above; Lady's Mantle a beautiful and useful plant particularly for hormonal balance.

Basic Seaweed Knowledge

Seaweed or Marine Vegetables are super rich foods and all seaweed in the UK are edible; **but always identify each one you pick.** Most seaweed holds an array of vitamins and minerals and are usually high in protein. Natural seaweed is a great way of restoring Iodine levels, Selenium and Magnesium which have become depleted in modern soils because of farming techniques.

Please also go to page 137 to 138 to read a summary of Doumeizel's book The Seaweed Revolution and how this magical Algae could be the answer to many of our environmental issues we face today.

I would definitely recommend Rachel Lambert's book *'Seaweed Foraging In Cornwall And The Isles of Scilly,' as a simple reference or* **Seaweeds of Britain and Ireland by** Francis Bunker

Colours; There are **3 colours of seaweed; brown, green and red and it has been said that their colour indicates their nutrional value** . The Greens show their link between the ocean and land plants they contain chlorophyll and essential fatty acids. Thin sheets of sea lettuce and hollow tubes of Gutweed characterise this group. **Red or purple** contain high levels of protein and are manufactured in jellies, ice creams and Laver bread. **Brown** seaweeds harvested to produce alginic acid used in medicine, a good source of iodine, Vitamin C, Beta-carotene and B12.

Seaweed should not be collected from the beach but carefully snipped from clean non polluted rock pools, or rocks which the tide regularly covers. There are two reason s for this

1. Seaweed gets all its nutrients from the sea so it has no roots just facilities to attach itself to the rock called 'Holdfasts.' Its soil is the abundant nutrients

of the sea. This however does mean that is absorbs all its surroundings, so if the sea is polluted it will absorb the pollution around it. Here at Marazion there is a sewage pipe so more ideal places to collect seaweed is straight from the rock pools at Gwithian or further West on The Lizard peninsula.

2. On the beach seaweed is not alive anymore so a lot of its nutrients may have disappeared and if it is a polluted area it may have absorbed the pollution.

Everyday food; you can rinse seaweed and add it to many meals. Some people like to dry it out and **The Cornish Seaweed Company** sell bags of dried seaweed that you can sprinkle on your salad, if you do not fancy gathering and drying it out.

When you gather seaweed rinse off and get as much sand out as possible then dry them out in a dryer or spread out on trays and pop in your greenhouse on a warm day. The next day you will have shrunken dried seaweed; you can then crumble this and blend it to use in soups and salads.

Medicinally; All seaweeds are **Superfoods; high in Antioxidants, Iodine as well as an array of vitamins and minerals. They are anti-inflammatory, anti-cancer, anti-diabetic and are often used for weight loss.**

The Wracks

Bladderwrack (*Fucus vesiculosus) and* **Eggwrack (***Ascophyllum nodosum); The bladders on both Egg Wrack and Bladder Wrack hold air so they can float and absorb minerals and nutrients from the air and the sea. As well as exchanging nutrients they provide shelter for sea life.*

Look out for a little fine semi parasitic sea weed known as **Sea Truffle or 'Mermaids pubes,'** *which attaches to the Wrack. It is really tasty when dried.*

Wrack are are best picked in Autumn, they can be a bit slimy during summer as they reproduces around the time.

Family Foragers in Cornwall operate most of their courses in the Autumn and winter as reproduction season over the Summer can mean the seaweed is extra slimy..I am sharing some basic seaweeds here but there are over 800 types and my suggestion is go on a specialist walk if you want to learn more varieties. The picking times does seem to vary with different foragers.

Caragreen /Irish Moss (Chondrus crispus); Like purple branches and best foraged in December and January. This is used as a thickener in many foods from puddings to pet food.

Medicinally it is still mixed with milk and honey in Scotland, Ireland and Venezuela.Used generally to help with coughs and cold, bronchial infection and congestion; has anti viral properties.

Dulse (Palmaria palmate);One of the most nutritious of the seaweeds rich in potassium and iodine as well as an array of vitamins and minerals, Dulse is full of Antioxidants and it has been likened to the taste of bacon. Dry out to add to salads or stir fry.

Gutweed (*Ulva instetinalis*) Mermaid's Hair. This is the very slippy one that covers the rocks with its fine green strands giving a grass appearance. It is really high in Iodine , iron and Magnesium for one. Dry and fry this lovely seaweed with salt, pepper and soya sauce as a starter or part of a stir fry.

Kelp(*Laminara digitata.*) Growth slows after summer so best to pick before summer ends. Highly nutritious and Penzance bay literally has a Kelp forest which is believed to sit over the stumps of an old ancient forest that existed when sea levels were lower. Kelp forests have the highest carbon capture than any other seaweed put together.

Kelp is full of minerals and vitamins and has a high Iodine content, great for Thyroid but don't over do as it may aggravate some Thyroid conditions.

Make crisps by wiping some of the slime off and hanging on the line in the Sun till they become crispy as The Devon Forager showed me.

Bootlace weed *(Chorda filum) Mermaid Tresses. May not see this one but have included purely because it's green thick noodle appearance is easy to identify.* It can reach up to eight metres, and is rich in age-halting and cancer-busting antioxidants. Like a lot of seaweed you can throw in a stir fry with onion garlic, ginger and soya sauce.

Pepper Dulse (Osmundea pinnatifida) A tiny dulse that is super tasty. Can become a greenish yellow colour the more exposed to sun it has been but generally holds a reddy/purple colour, known as the '**Truffle Of The Sea**,' It is high in Omega 3 and 6 and particularly noted for its anti oxidant effect and like all sea weeds can be a valuable tool for weight loss and a great anti inflammatory.

Sea Lettuce (*Ulva lactuca*) is very thin almost translucent and delicate and has high photosynthesis action and so has been known utilize nitrates and phosphates quickly turning them into a nutritious form. It has therefore been used as a filter for water systems and aquariums, It is full of vitamin, minerals , proteins and fats. It tastes good dried out or in raw form but for obvious reason please do not pick from polluted sites and like all sea weeds pick off the rocks in clean rock pool.

Sea Spaghetti (Himanthalia elongate) *Known as 'Spinach Of The Sea,' as well as Iodine Sea Spaghetti is high in Alganites which locks moisture into the skin to creating a glow. Also high in Calcium and Magnesium, so great for Depression , Menopause and Heart health, use like spaghetti but not in mass quantities.*

A lovely illustration above by Y Scott of some of the seaweeds I mentioned.

Above; A morning collection from Godrevy, ready to be dried out; Bladder Wrack, Sea Lettuce and some ' Mermaid's Pubes' (Syphon Weed.)

Extraordinary names in the foraging and healing world of past and present.

There are many extraordinary people in the movements of natural health but here are just a few that really stand out for me;

Ann Wigmore (1909 -1994); An extraordinary up bringing in war torn Europe (Please see my write up on Grass), Anne Wigmore came to the USA and not only brought her herbal roots her grandmother had taught her but set up a healing sanctuary with the use of Grass. She was also famous for setting up The Hippocrates movement which is in full flow today as an ' alternative' (*) movement in North America. **(*)Alternative in because pre 1930s plants were main stream medicine till allopathic was announced as being the mainstream health treatments.**

Dr Maynard Murray (1911-1984); *Charles Walter's books 'Fertility From The Ocean Deep,' really covers the great work of Maynard Murray. As a medical Doctor in the 1930s Murray was increasingly concerned about the rising rates of preventable disease in humans. Murray really was the inventor of the phrase 'you are what you eat.' His studies link to the connection between the sea and health and the fact that most of the earth (as high as Mount Everest) shows fossilized records that they have been covered with sea at some point; so our soil and our plants still have elements of the sea's nutrients in their makeup. The 102 elements of the sea showed perfect balance and harmony whist the soils that were being over farmed and just given the hefty macro nutrients (NPK) did not have the fine balance of macro and micro nutrients to transport into the plants we eat and this short fall was causing disease. This in turn invited in disease and the need for toxic rescue. In his words 'short circuited life's electrical systems.' This links up to books like 'The Invisible Rainbow.'*

Dr Maynard Murray's most important work was the autopsies of sea creatures compared to river fish. The sea creatures showed no sign of disease and their arterial systems and organs showed no difference compared to new born calves. His fascination with the perfect balance the sea held and its ability to cleanse itself became his life's work. He experimented using small amounts of dried sea weed to fertilise crops and despite many hold backs his research showed significant improvement in yields and nutritional quality of the crop as well as improvement in the animals that ate crops that had been fertilised in this way, for example pigs did not need to eat the root of the plant when they were fed the more nutritious crops.

Juliette de Bairacli Levy; Also know as 'Julia Of The Herb.' (1912-2009) Renowned for her skills for her skill with animals a jewish born Brit who became a fully qualified as a vet, but disillusioned with the treatments and out comes of pharmacology , she began to write about herbal remedies for our pets. She became respected by farmers in Scotland when she saved many Sheep from famine and disease through her treatment of Molasses and ground ivy. She left Britain and travelled alongside gypsies in Europe for 60 years with her beloved Afghan hounds, she also had two children during this time. In her book; *'Common Herbs for Natural Health'* starts with these two sentences; **Herbal medicine is man's natural medicine: The powers of herbs cannot be denied."**

Massanobu Fukuoka (1913 -2008) The founder of natural farming and author of 'The One Straw Revolution,' and 'Sewing Seeds In The Dessert,' Fukuoka's ideas are starting to sing louder in a world that has destroyed one of the most important living tools we have with modern agriculture; our soil. Fukuoka spent most of his life studying the way in which nature works and he worked alongside it to produce greater yields than his neighbouring farms who were using traditional methods.

Maurice Messegue(1921 – 2017) a Frenchman who not only learned but inherited his Father's skills as a healer in a French peasant community. After his Father was killed in a tragic accident Messegue took up his Father's practice and travelled across France. At first he was not noticed amongst the communities he was offering his herbal remedies to, but once he miraculously cured a couple of people, including an alcoholic tramp with Eczema, word spread like wild fire and over years Messegue was working with the rich and famous on a world wide scale including high rankers like Winston Churchill. He was of great threat to the medical profession and regularly got taken to court, always supported by the people he had healed. His remedies were a series of herbal hand and foot baths taken daily over a few days or weeks.

Nicholas Culpeper 1616 -1654. Born into gentry studied at Cambridge which he abandoned after his fiancée got struck by lightning and died! He then worked with the poor and often didn't charge. He also published his studies and knowledge in English as opposed to the conventional Latin. Died from TB possibly because of an old war wound and smoking habit. Infuriated the medical establishment.

Nicole Pelian present day American anthropologist, herbalist and mother. Has spent years living and studying indigenous people after her own diagnosis of MS in 2000 and being resigned to a wheelchair she got herself back to wellness by practicing what she preaches and her book 'The Lost Book Of Herbal Remedies,' and her courses give astonishing and inspiring advice.

Rachel Carson (1907 – 1964) A Scientist with a background in Biology and an ability to write about nature in an extraordinary poetic way; a modern day Einstein; a pioneer who paved the way for everyday people to question our right not to be poisoned by industry. She also became fascinated by the sea and her book **'The Sea Around Us'** is a work of magic that seems to describe the wonder of the universe, the power of the great moon pulling the energies of the tides. When she produced her astonishing book 'Silent Spring,' attacking credibly and beautifully the use of DDT, she was also attacked by Industry with an attempt to discredit her as a woman and an exceptional Scientists. Time only revered and grew her popularity beyond her untimely death and today we are living in the chemical soup she so passionately wrote about. Coleburn's book (below) was seen as a follow up to the warning Carson had given the world and both these women should be honoured as Heroes of their time and let's hope their messages will be acted upon sooner rather than later; Big industry is destroying the natural world!

Theo Coleburn(1927-2014); 'Our Stolen Future.' A great pioneer about chemicals in our food system and how the human foetus was becoming more contaminated. Her research linked poor health with the increasing use of plastics. She also spoke about EDCs ..**Endocrine Disruptive Chemicals** pointing to the harm processed foods put onto the human with such vigour their reactions could imitate various hormones leaving the body's natural systems, particularly the Endocrine system, to become dysfunctional. Before her death she wrote a letter to Obama who was the president of the USA about her concerns. This is well documented in her book 'Our Stolen Future.' One of Ray's favourites.

Dr Zach Bush; Jumped ship from traditional medicine to inspirational talks on the loss of human health from chemicals and modern health systems. His talks are shocking but inspirational about the mass health decline of both the human body and the world we live in. He gives us hope through his teachings about the power of the human spirit, the miracle of the microbiome and the ability of our bodies to heal themselves given the right conditions. His Roundup facts are shocking as are the rates of disease and Autism epidemic in the modern world.

Other points of Interest to explore; Sun cancer rates have increased since the intro of suncream..absorption of Vitamin D directly from the sun is vital to our existence exposure to the sun reduces the risk of 70% of cancers..most people who get skin cancer are in the sun more so use more sunscreen containing reactive substances that become carcinogenic when exposed to the sun. Zinc oxide, Titanium Dioxide and Aluminium Hydroxide to name a few. Let your sun absorb the sun and cover up when you have had enough. There are also natural options without The Zinc Oxide.

Our Haemoglobin in our body is only 1 chemical away from chloroplasts in plants and the way we absorb energy and O2 from the atmosphere..the difference is we use Iron a plant uses Magnesium..all the products of carbon.

Wild soul.

Edibles placed on my table that they thought I might like

Not out of date, not even ripe!

A red pepper; organic from Archie Browns, that you would no longer use.

Some hummus you might have tucked into before your afternoon snooze.

But there was some Cornish dried seaweed you would spread on 15 wild leaves

Picked from your wild sanctuary, tweed jacket off then rolled up your sleeves.

You'd have thought of Maynard Murray who spoke of rich nutrients from the sea

No weeds, leaves embedded with its minerals; how all food should be!

Or Renne Quinton whose studies they hide

Had replaced blood for sea water and saved many lives.

No conformity or rows no sprays like vegetables now

Our ownership, our downfall (like Zach Bush says) started all with the plough!

You would have told me of Fukuoka who watched for five years

The land taking shape naturally to produce better yields.

Yet you yourself were your own One Straw Revolution.

Turned Sand into soil with sea weed and toil; a natural solution.

For you Ray, were also a pioneer of the natural world

You searched every wild corner and read every word.

And there you would find Julia of the herbs another hero who was never acknowledged,

A British Vet who travelled with wild folk and healed with the herbs that she foraged.

And there in your cottage situated at the top up the lane

Your forest garden would bring back all their teachings together again.

Yet these perishables on my table would have you perish before their decline was complete

They remained fresh a long way past your heart took its last beat.

And I will cry with the Sea Beet who will miss you singing its praises

And the plants you most cherished , the Dandelions, the Nettles , the Michaelmas Daisies.

For no one needs supplements when the best nutrients surround us and are free

As Synopolous stated they contain the omegas the minerals, all the vitamins like B,C and D.

But I will never forget you taught me of the big beasts that tore out natures's soul

So far were they from the wilderness of wild and how ironic that it was your heart they stole!

They lose though, when Nature receives you amongst its great Ether.

But I will miss you amongst soft Mullein, the Sow Thistle and you as my teacher.

Hedgerows will weep the loss amongst the plants you love most.

Where your presence is always, on this peninsula along this Cornish coast.

EM Jan24.

Make Nature your friend Again!

Ray was vey interested in the chemical soup we live in and the pioneers who spoke about it and if there was a base for all his research it would come from **Raymond Fitzgerald in his fascinating book 'The Hundred year lie.'** (2006.) At the beginning of the book he presents this quote;

'We are surrounded everyday by invisible sea of synthetic chemicals, and our bodies absorb them like sponges until we are toxic.

We consume foods that have been depleted of essential natural healing nutrients. These nutrients have been replaced by synthetic chemical additives.

These additives in our processed foods interact synergistically in our bodies with synthetic chemicals absorbed from our water, our air and our consumer products, weakening our immune systems.

Once weakened, we become susceptible to illnesses disease that medical practitioners treat with synthetic chemical drug compounds that often prove even more toxic.

And this cycle in our culture and in our lives repeats itself over and over.'

Please see the following articles overleaf;

Ray's articles;Grass, Mother sea and our need to get back to the natural world.

Content;

Enzymes page 115; Dr Howell/ sprouting seeds.

Grass page 116-117;Benefits and Ann Wigmore.

Biocide page 118-119 Mitochondria and death of the human cell.

Mother Earth; programmed for life; 119; Dr David Barker chemicals in the womb.

Earth's Maternity Care page 119-120; Barker and Chutkan, the microbiome.

Reconnecting With The Sea; page 120-121 Rachel Carson and our microbiome.

Grass – For The Forgiveness Of Nature ...page 121-122; The Buffalo and grass juice.

Mother Sea and the stream of life page 122-123; Renee Quinton our blood and the sea.

Mother Sea; those who stayed and those who left page 123-124; Martin Murray and his work with sea mammals the man who invented 'You are what you eat.'

The Fight To Retain Our Natural Selves page 124; Theo Coleburn; chemicals in the human body.

Our Natural Legacy; Page 125-126; Raymomnd Fitzgerald 'The hundred Year Lie.'

There's Something In The Air page 126-127; 5G and EMFs.

Meanwhile At The Top Of The Chain:127.Electro smog and EMF damage.

Eat Dirt And Thrive page 127; Intro to Zach Bush.

The Special Relationship page 128;,;Howard and Balfour; The Microbiome and plants.

Enzymes

David Barker showed how the developing foetus in the womb depended at each stage of growth on the nutrients in the Mother's blood, and Maynard Murray identified these as a whole spectrum of 90 minerals in balance with each other and similar in constitution to seawater. What gives life to what otherwise would be seen to be a lifeless arrangement of chemicals of chemicals had become the subject of a 50 year investigation by an American Doctor Edward Howell. Together with presenting us with our own set of digestive bacteria for our gut, one of the final acts of the Mother in giving birth is the charging of our 'enzyme battery' which enables the new born to power all its metabolic functions from moving its toes to thinking its thoughts. Dr Howell asserts that this charge has to last a lifetime in this axiom. 'The length of life is inversely proportional to the rate of exhaustion of the enzyme potential.' One further , if unwelcome, piece of news is that cooking will destroy enzymes and that the resulting overburdened load on the digestive enzymes will reduce the metabolic enzyme potential. Another piece of more recent research indicates the dependence of enzymes on the presence of trace elements as 'keys' in order to unlock their potentials.

It has long been acknowledged that the greatest production of enzymes in in the newly sprouted seeds and the work of the Kentons, in bringing this to the attention of a large number of people created a huge interest in the growing of sprout gardens in the 1980s. Bringing Murray's work alongside Howell's discoveries we can create enhanced sprout gardens irrigated with dilute seawater, enabling the seeds to take whatever minerals they require in order to fulfil their potential. I have used 2000ppm of Himalayan salt solution in the illustrated gardens.

Cutting the tops of carrots, parsnips and beetroots at half an inch and immersing a quarter inch depth of seawater with the occasional change of liquid will produce several nutritious cuts of vegetables throughout winter. The whole syatem is both an excellent way to reduce the burden on one enzyme' account and a wonderful way to connect children to the delights of the living world.

I love two of Dr Howells stories from nature. The habit of squirrels burrowing nuts to start their enzyme production, and retrieving them later in their newly activated condition. The other is about the practice of Swallows, mainly insect eating birds, preparing for their long migrations by filling their crops with seeds which will keep both their 'engines,' and 'sat-navs,' powered as the energy giving enzymes are slowly released during germination on their long journeys.

One way of dealing with what is usually a heavy drain on the enzyme account over Christmas could be to soak all those nuts for 24hours before eating there by turning a deficit on the metabolic account into credit.

Ref; Enzyme Nutrition' by Dr Edward Howell.

GRASS

Said to be the oldest, most widespread and most nutritious plant on earth, with 4,700 varieties from 100ft high bamboos down to 1". Covering 30% of the land surface including both the Arctic and Antarctic it feeds most of the largest mammals.

It has been claimed to supply a complete food. Of the world's 102 elements grass has been assessed to provide 92 of them, exactly the same as in human blood plasma. In order to make a complete protein our bodies require 22, 14 of which the body is able to produce, the other 8 to be consumed in food, and grass contains all of them. Even the juices alone contain the amino acids. One American grassland expert has expressed surprise that grass hasn't been studied as a potential food for humans, capable of supporting a body from birth to a prime old age. The same researcher quoted the case of a Kansas lawyer whom together with a wife and three children, lived solely on grass for 3 years. Also the case of the English doctor Barbara Noore who walked from Los Angeles to New York and lived on grass along the route.

The most impressive evidence for the nutritional and therapeutic value of grass has been contained in the story of Anne Wigmore who as a child living in Lithuania, witnessed healing both directly and indirectly through the work of her grandmother, a natural healer. Later, in America, when she was advised to have both her legs removed above the ankle after the onset of gangrene following an accident, she healed herself using green plants, mainly grass. She later set up a hostel receiving desperately ill individuals on whom mainstream medicine had given up, treating them with wheatgrass juice. The practice still continues in the Hippocrates Health Institute of Florida.
Testimonies as to the acceptability of grass in human food had shown that it was being proposed to supplement flour by adding ground dried grass after successful trials in Canada.
A personal testimony has been recorded as follows-

'By devoting attention to the careful drying of grass into hay, I have been able to dry it artificially, so when I was eating my repast, consisting of hay with other ingredients, I appeared to myself, to be the most delightful meal, that was pervaded by the taste and aroma of new mown hay. In like manner, in cutting up and mixing with freshly cut grass mowings, the petals of roses and lettuce leaves, and fruit, adding sugar to my taste, I have been able to make myself delicious salads. I have also been able by adding cut-up rose leaves to make a salad which consisted of fresh grass, rolled oats, sugar, and half an ounce of currants, to produce a meal which gave me the sense that I was enjoying a repast which had the taste and the aroma of fresh leeshees, an Egyptian fruit of the most delicate and delicious flavour'.
(J.R.B. Branson).

Importance of grass in vegetarian and vegan diets
Meat and dairy consumers have the benefit of a potent detoxifier and a key anti-cancer substance, conjugated linoleic acid (CLA) which also promotes lean muscles, strength, enhances metabolism, and boosts immunity. It derives from grass and is only present in the

animals that feed from them. Vegetarians and vegans are advised to include grass in their diets – grass juice being its most convenient form

A version of this nutritious and therapeutic juice for home use can be produced by using wild grass or sprouted wheat grass juiced with lemon and apple -

    1 cup of grass cut into 1" pieces   1 lemon

    1 apple   4 cups water

Choose young grass if possible, but if wild grass is too old to chew, it can be blended into a juice. Gather a handful of grass from outside or from your indoor trays of wheatgrass. Cut the blades into 1" pieces. Add directly into the blender. Add one apple (sliced) and the juice of one lemon, and four cups of water. Blend thoroughly and strain the green juice. Drink the juice while it is fresh.

I choose wild grass and blend with an apple in a masticating juicer rather than a centrifugal juicer thereby giving higher levels of antioxidants in the juice.

Raymond Yarwood 2019

Biocide?

In 1974 a self-confessed biology watcher, Dr Lewis Thomas, wrote in "The Lives of a Cell" –"We are not made up, as we had always supposed, of successively enriched packets of our own parts. We are shared, rented, occupied. At the interior of our cells, driving them, providing the oxidated energy that sends us out for the improvement of each shining day, are the mitochondria, and in a strict sense they are not ours. They are as much symbionts as the rhizobial bacteria in the roots of beans. Without them, we would not move a muscle, drum a finger, think a thought. Mitochondria are stable and responsible lodgers and I choose to trust them. My cells are no longer the pure line entities I was raised with; they are ecosystems more complex than Jamaica Bay. I like to think they work in my interest, that each breath they draw for me, but perhaps it is they who walk through the local park in the early morning, sensing my senses, listening to my music, thinking my thoughts.

I am consoled, somewhat, by the thought that the green plants are in the same fix.

(It is estimated that the human body has twenty three thousand genes, plus a microbiome of five to ten million genes. The source of all life on earth is said to be the sea which has a population of microbes representing 50 to 90 per cent of the ocean's biomass. This is said to be equivalent to the weight of two hundred and forty billion African elephants. While irrigation of the land by modern farming is producing a drain on the world's soil estimated to have no more than another 49 years, we are also being reminded of the benefits of tsunamis and hurricanes in re-fertilising the land. Colonies of microbes are said to live in the clouds and they help to form cirrus clouds and form the nucleus of snowflakes and rain. They influence both weather and climate as well as recycle nutrients and decompose pollutants – recently it has been discovered that microbes have adapted to feed on plastic turning it to a harmless substance.)

Present day researchers are grouping all living creatures as inter-reactive communities of microbes known as microbiomes. The WIFI cloud is said to be already interfering with life's fundamental programme. There is already good evidence that mitochondria are failing the human sperm. Estimates are that fewer of today's boys will ever be able to become fathers and reports from the USA are that one in six couples are not able to conceive. Evidence also shows that insects are experiencing reproductive problems. On challenging our local MP and Government Minister about the inadvisability of intensifying radiation in our atmosphere without taking note of the rising volume of research. I was told that the UK plans to lead the world in 5G by 2027. Researchers in the know have described this as insanity.
Raymond Yarwood – summer 2019

Mother Earth – Programmed for Life
With the total cost of caring both for the young and elderly as brain diseases are on the rise, investigators are comparing the costs of returning to the care for life that nurtured us for thousands of years against the rising social and economic costs we face today.

It is only recently that an investigation into the purpose of the appendix to the intestine by investigators at Duke University USA has paved the way for a more complete understanding of how our bodies work. The removal of the appendix to the intestines has for years been done in the belief that it served no function and had become a useless bit of the organ left over from evolution. These researchers have now claimed that '*The appendix serves as a safe haven for useful bacteria when illness flushes those bacteria from the rest of the intestines, and later helps to re-boot the system*'.

The use of computer language appears to get us a long way in our understanding of the operating systems within our bodies, and carrying on using the same language, we can investigate what is hacking into these long evolved and programmed systems.

Earth's Maternity Care
When Dr David Barker concluded his fifteen year study of the development of the baby in the womb with his book 'Nutrition in the Womb' in 2008 he had identified the crucial role of the placenta in providing an 'on time' delivery service of nutrients from the mother's body as the different organs of the baby began to develop. Absence of these at the appropriate time, he claimed, could lead to heart disease, diabetes and stroke in later life. He further claimed that *Green leafy vegetables have been shown to increase babies' birthweights. They have a greater effect on birthweight than would be expected from the growth-promoting substances, such as folic acid and iron that they are known to contain.*

A more recent investigator takes the story further. Dr Robynne Chutkan in her book 'The Microbiome Solution' of 2015 reveals that further systems, programmed to ensure the delivery of a baby equipped to handle the hazards that its new environment presents, begin in the mother's gut garden nourishing the trillions of microbes that when called upon carry out Nature's programmes.

In preparing for the delivery of a baby well equipped to enter the world from the nurture and protection of the mother's womb, the researcher tells us that during pregnancy the mother's body attracts bacteria from her gut garden onto the walls of the birth canal by secreting glycogen causing the microbes to multiply which in turn excrete lactic acid keeping potential invaders at bay. During normal delivery the baby turns and head down collects this protective coat and brushes the mother's anus as it enters the world bringing nose and mouth in contact as it in turn collects the seeding of its own micro floral garden for its own digestive tract. At the same time other bacteria from mother's garden are busy turning her indigestible breast milk into a form easily assimilated by the newly born baby. While this is going on further bacteria have arrived to protect the nipple of the breast from harmful microbes. In both cases of these natural processes, industrial chemicals in the mother's gut or on her skin, are being seen to corrupt the natural working of nature's systems.

Dr Barker had earlier concluded his study with the words *Today in the western world mothers should trust nature and enter pregnancy with confidence* .Researchers are now uncovering where this confidence should lie.

A new and exciting field of investigation has opened up as our understanding of the way our own micro floral garden relates to that of the Earth's, returning to the ancient belief in Earth as mother, as the universal caring service..

Reconnecting with the Sea is our best hope of survival

The strains of 'We do like to be besides the sea' will have died and those people along the sand who in the words of poet Robert Frost had turned their back on the land and looked at the sea all day, will have returned to their homes. Why the attraction of the sea? A closer look at who had spent those hours in the deck chair takes us nearer to an answer. With scientists able to examine the minute of living systems known as an individual's'microbiomes' we as humans bring the whole of our close knit family of 23,000 genes that are said to be human and our ever present 'household 'of between 5 and 10 million genes of accompanying microbes wherever we go. If the human genes were vapourised it is said that the image left behind would still be recognised as human, the extent of their coverage would still be visible reclining in the chair. Could the seaside attraction be that they felt that they needed to return to the source of the deal that they had struck along with all land creatures to keep in touch when they left the sea for the land, as revealed in Rachel Carson's book 'The sea around us'. We on land had undertaken to keep a salty flowing stream in our bodies which we passed on from generation to generation. As humans we arranged that each new born should begin life in its mother's replica of the ocean for around nine months before receiving the salty stream on birth which would continue to supply nourishment for the rest of life. The sea on her part had continued to provide nourishment to our food sources, plant or animal also dependent on connection with the sea, and recent researchers have returned from their airship laboratories in the clouds with knowledge on how the sea has continued to do this. Researchers along Carson's 'salty stream of life' have discovered that all living creatures consist of a microbiome workforce of minute creatures dominated by bacteria, the tiny workforce that attends living creatures, constructing, demolishing, protecting, and energising, with their materials the minerals. The sea holds a full complement of both workers and materials, the largest of earth's microbiomes. Every raindrop, we are told, that falls from a cloud arising over the sea contains a microbe or a mineral, in order to build or sustain life below.

This salty stream, started in the sea and undisturbed provides the richness seen in the tropical rainforests. As we cut down rainforests we are beginning to see responses from 'Mother Sea' in

order to keep her side of the deal, but disastrous to modern civilisation, as recently pointed out in a paper in a North American journal under the heading
'The gift of natural disasters to replenish soils.' This article tries to explain why areas visited by hurricanes, floods and tsunamis leave behind more fertile lands. It also points out that the rise of modern civilisation depended on the flooding of rivers such as the Nile to sustain growing populations
The University of Hawai'i is leading the way in demonstrating how there is an instant, simple, universal, and sustainable way to recover the health of the earth and its inhabitants through a closer relationship with the sea and to turn our preoccupation with extinction Into one of renewal.
Raymond Yarwood
Phillack
Published in The Cornishman September 19th 2019

Grass – For the Forgiveness of Nature –
The Constant Benediction

The above quote could be mistaken for many of those down the ages including those from the bible, 'all flesh is grass', 'he was advised to eat grass like the oxen', 'their eyes did fail because there was no grass'. Reference to 'green pastures and still waters' is my favourite.
The quote in the heading however is from none other than a politician. Senator John Ingalls from Kansas recorded a tribute to the blue grass of the prairies one late afternoon in 1871 as he looked out on the rolling acres that had supported miles long herds of buffalos. Their bountiful ecology is only just being appreciated after the buffalo had been slaughtered for recreation, and the land had been 'turned upside down' in the words of Native Americans, with the resulting dust blown all the way to the Capitol, leaving the water table in a critical state as aquifiers were driven into the earth in the quest to regain fertility.
Grass up to the first joint is said to be sweet and fast growing and acts as a carbon pump under grazing conditions, the animals taking the succulent stem before moving on. The cow pats are then colonised by dung beetles feeding off them followed by a growing population of worms and microbes leaving not only a nutrient rich soil but a fibrous matt that allows for the slow filtering of rainwater as it adds to the groundwater without runoff.
Biologists are claiming an even closer relationship between ourselves and the grasses. A riddle that some take pleasure in posing refers to the tree of life which has grown to the form of a bush as more and more microscopic families are added. 'If we humans are positioned at 8 o'clock – who is our nearest neighbour?'
Most people are bemused by the answer which turns out to be – grasses!
The more we study the relationship, the clearer it becomes. Grass is both rich in chlorophyll with only one atom difference, magnesium in plants and iron in human blood. Grass of all plants can provide our total need in minerals and trace elements. Most importantly, whichever diet we adopt – omnivorous, vegetarian or vegan we are being told that we need to incorporate grass in our diet. Kim Evans a writer on natural health topics states in an article in the American publication Natural News that all of us need contact with grass in our diets. She states that 'Conjugated linoleic acid CLA is a key antioxidant substance. It promotes lean muscle mass and strength

while enhancing metabolism. It also boosts immunity and its scarcity in other sources is actually the reason why some health authors promote animal consumption. But where does CLA come from? It's in the grass that animals eat – and it's not in many other foods, even other greens. In fact, if you're not drinking grass juice or consuming animal products, you're probably not getting enough CLA in your diet .But how better to get your CLA than going to the source – the grass.' Kim Evans March 21 2011.
I have tried wild grass juice blended with an apple with different people and we all find the drink delicious.
Charles Walters Executive Director of Acres USA the mecca and publishing house for Organic America, seemed to be obsessed with grass and its relationship with the sea. The sea is the starting place for all life on earth and grass is its nearest relative on land.
And still the grass eter
Where castles stood and grandeur died
From "The flitting" by John Clare.   Raymond Lockdown April 2020

Mother Sea and the Stream of Life
Well known for her book *Silent Spring* Rachel Carson was already well read and respected for her books about the sea. In the *The Sea Around Us* written in 1950 she had divided the book into three sections, the first one headed 'Mother Sea' in which she wrote, 'When they went ashore the animals that took up a land life took with them a part of the sea in their bodies, a heritage which they passed on to their children and which even today links each land animal with its origin in the ancient sea. Fish, amphibian, and reptile, warm bloodied bird and mammal – each of us carries in our vein a salty stream…'
Years earlier Rene Quinton working in France had carried out experiments in 1904, on stray dogs brought to him, to test his theory that by replacing this salty stream, the blood plasma, with sea water, would have a therapeutic value, and could be applied to humans. The dogs own plasma was exhausted through their kidneys as the ocean plasma was infused. The dogs not only thrived but appeared to be healthier. Shortly after recording success in his animal experiments, France was in the grip of an epidemic of babies dying from an intestinal infection. Quinton set up a dispensary and such was the success of the treatment that soon there were 10 clinics where physicians had helped save thousands of lives by the time the epidemic had passed.(please watch the documentary- Rene Quinton- The Seawater Cure of All Diseases, on U-tube) A fuller summary of the value of Quinton's work is included in 'Fertility from the ocean deep by Charles Walters of Acres USA .I quote -
The conclusions established by this 19th Century worker have a validity of maximum interest to farmers, nutritionists, physicians and the people called patients. All organisms can be considered an aquaculture filled with a liquid called the primary ocean. All the cells of the body require this bath. When the quality of the bath changes, cellular nutrition is destroyed. This in plant, animal, and mankind. This undermines the defences of plant, animal and mankind against pathogens. Therefore to opt for health is to opt for the restoration of the liquid envelope in which plants, animals and human beings live. There are no secrets in Nature, only a failure to see what we look at.
Dr Maynard Murray, in the 1930s, a hard pressed American G.P. had the habit of relaxing after a busy work schedule by watching the landing of fish at the nearby harbour. Curious to discover

why the fish seemed to be in good health led him on a 30year long journey of discovery, where he discovered that while some river fish suffered from cancer, there was no sign in the fish he regularly observed from the sea. During a long sea journey of investigation he also discovered that an adult whale's cells were no different from those of her calf. .Here he claimed was the elusive fountain of youth and the keys were the trace elements fed upon by the microorganisms in the animal's food reasoned Murray.

Discovering that our blood, when healthy, contained 92 elements of the 102 present in seawater, he set about analysing the content of plants – grass came top of the list with 92, like ourselves, sweet potatoes 70, tomatoes 54. By bringing seawater ashore and applying to crops in diluted form, he claimed to have discovered the ultimate fertiliser.

Now largely ignored as in the case of Rene Quinton, a revival of interest is taking place through the increasing attention that is being shown to what is happening to our own microbes when our body is missing any one of the elements now understood to be an essential part of Rachel Carson's 'salty stream',. While research shows how far down we are in minerals in our soils, therefore our food, this is being related to the lack of the ancient microbes and a subsequent decrease in our health, leading to many of the so called modern chronic diseases Recent research at The College of Tropical Agriculture and Human Resources, University of Hawaii has produced a report 2013 Natural Farming: Diluted Seawater (available on the internet). 'Mother sea' is around us bearing all of the ingredients of the important stream of life referred to by Rachel Carson

Raymond Yarwood – September 2019

Mother Sea – Those who stayed and those who left

As chronic diseases began to be recorded in the U.S.A., with cancer rates having risen from 3% of all recorded deaths in 1905, rising to 30% by the end of the century, in the early 30s Dr Maynard Murray a hard pressed physician relaxed each day by watching the local fishermen landing their catch. He brought with him the concerns of his profession with a caseload of patients suffering from cancer, diabetes, arthritis, osteoporosis, arteriosclerosis, and other degenerative diseases weighing on his shoulders. His curiosity as a scientist soon contrasted the healthy population of the fishermen's catch with his daily contact with humans. This began a 30 year's investigation of the comparative health of sea, freshwater, and land based animals.
(*Before summarising some of Dr Murray's discoveries I would like to quote an excerpt from Dr Henry Schroeder's book Trace Elements and Man published in 1973*)

"From those accounts we can see that when vertebrates decided to invade the ocean's shores, those of their chemical systems depending on bulk and trace elements, were evolutionary fixed, and there was no need to develop them much further. The proper amounts of trace elements were present in seawater, not too much and not too little. There was a problem with excess of bulk elements which had been solved by gill, gut and kidney, and a problem with excesses of trace metals, early solved by the hepatopancreas, and plenty of food was at hand.

There seemed to be no earthly reason why they should not be complacent and happy in the environment where they had evolved. But they were not. They chose or were forced to invade the land." (*My emphasis*)

Dr Murray's curiosity led him to suspend his medical practice and hire a trawler and crew to explore the oceans and its larger inhabitants. Tissue samples from an adult 50 - 90 year old and her calf showed no aging in the adult whale. This side of his research convinced him that the ever present salty environment of the sea was conducive to longevity in its inhabitants.

His second and major discovery when brought to the attention of Dr Edward Howell a lifelong researcher in enzyme nutrition, was greeted with the comments that 'these highly illuminating discoveries would have a profound bearing on health and disease' and was included as an appendix to his book Enzyme Nutrition – Unlocking the secrets of eating right for health, vitality and longevity.' *See below the summary of Dr Murray's findings as reported*

"Within the years 1942-45 under the auspices of Archer Daniel's Midland Company of Chicago, between 900-1000 sperm whales were dissected in Peru. The only pathology sought in these animals involved malignancy, atherosclerosis, and arthritis. None of these were found. We also measured the size of the thymus gland which persisted in these animals, weight 80 to 100 lbs in the slaughtered carcass. While microscopic sections of these glands were not numerous, however, the tissue examined showed them to be active and not replaced by fat or fibrous tissue. The coronary arteries microscopically did not show any atherosclerosis; neither did the aortas. There was approximately 8 inches of saturated subcutaneous fat in whales, yet no hardening of the arteries.

Off the Aleutian Islands of Alaska, around 3,000 seals were dissected for their fur. No malignant tumours were found, and there was no pathology in their arteries and joints. We dissected about 30 small harp seals which were slaughtered on ice floes off the western coast of Canada. These animals also showed no pathology of the kinds mentioned above."

Dr Maynard Murray then devoted the rest of his time to bringing ashore the benefits he had observed in the sea. Raymond Yarwood- 2020

The Fight to Retain our Natural Selves

Rachel Carson's book 'Silent Spring' will be remembered as a rallying cry for the many who were concerned at the effects that man-made chemicals were having on wildlife. I would suspect that fewer have heard of the work of Theo Colborne who 30yrs later, in 1997, alerted the world to dangers that were now posing a threat to humans, in her joint authored book, 'Our Stolen Future'. With no lower limit and the capacity to mimic and replace the body's natural hormones in our control system known as the 'endocrine system', virtually every aspect of our bodies was under threat from synthetic chemicals derived from the fossil fuel industry, introduced without regulation or testing. Under the greatest threat, she showed, was the baby in the womb in danger of being set on course for one of a number of disorders.(see Body Burden – Pollution of the
 Newborns. 2005). Theo Colborne died in 2014 at the age of 87 two years after sending an open letter to the President of the USA, making an impassioned plea that mirrored the letter of The National Cancer Institute 3yrs earlier, but setting out in great detail what these disorders that mothers and their babies were exposed to. Her letter can be seen on u-tube – TEDX, as **'Letter to the President about chemicals disrupting our bodies - 2012**. She hoped that her message would be listened to in millions of homes across the world.

More recently a presentation on u-tube by Barbara O'neil entitled 'Balancing your Hormones' sets out the important effects on the natural importance of hormones at different stages and times in the body

With the chemical industry worried about the future of their products, a new area known as 'Green Chemistry' is being explored. The new products will be tested for harmless recycling in

what has been dubbed the 'cycle economy' (sounds familiar – isn't that what we have been about all along in the organic movement?).
Raymond

Our Natural Legacy
"We can harness the power of positive, health –enhancing synergies from foods and herbs to strengthen our immune systems. Using food as medicine enables us to detoxify ourselves of chemical contaminants and cure ourselves of illness and disease.

An ancient legacy of naturally occurring health and healing is based on thousands of years of human experience with wisdom traditions that follow the principles of nature. These natural cures are being affirmed by Western medicine in laboratory experiments that show them to be more effective, less costly, and less toxic than most pharmaceutical drugs."

The Hundred Year Lie – How To Protect Yourself From Chemicals That Are Destroying Your Health – Randall Fitzgerald -2007

The Future is in the hands of Organic Growers and those who support them
There have been a number of responses across the world to Theo Colborn's letter to the President of the USA on the present dangers from the huge numbers of synthetic chemicals present in the environment. One of her main defences set out in her book 'Our Stolen Future' is as follows -
"Avoid animal fat as much as possible. As the journey of the PCB molecule demonstrated, many of these chemicals travel through the food web in fat and become more concentrated as they move upward to the top predators such as polar bears and humans. In a 1999 report, the U.S. Environmental Protection Agency found that meats and cheeses are a major source of dioxin exposure in the United States today. So eating less animal fat – found in foods such as butter, cheese ,lamb, beef and other meats – will greatly reduce exposure to hormone–disrupting chemicals. Again it is particularly important that women minimise the consumption of animal fat *from birth until the end of their childbearing years.* They bear the next generation and the responsibility to protect their children from contamination. Moreover a family diet rich in vegetables, grains, and fruits has a multigenerational benefit, for it will reduce the rate of heart disease and cancer for adults and may protect your children and grandchildren from prenatal hormone disruption.
Buy or raise your own organically grown fruit and vegetables. If they aren't available at your local supermarket, or are too expensive, look to see if your grocer offers produce that has been tested and been found to have 'no detectable residue'. Ask your grocer if the grocery chain screens its food for contaminants or buys from suppliers that do. You have the right to know what is in the food you buy. Encourage your grocers to stock and promote organic produce...."
This of course is America – but also the home of endocrine research where it has been discovered that no alien substance can be too small to disrupt the present integrity and future workings of our bodies through its major control system, the endocrine system. This needs to be compared with the predominant view of industry and regulators, based on a teaching from a 16th century Swiss physician Paracelsus, that has now become their outdated and out of touch mantra 'the dose makes the poison'.

See *Our Stolen Future – Theo Colborn, Dianne Dumanoski, and John Peterson Myers - 1999*

There's something in the Air
These are just a few of the recent reports in what is described as the greatest human experiment on the degrees of tolerance of all living systems, to the increasing electrification of the Earth's atmosphere

Bees harmed by mobiles at New Year.
A study closely correlating levels of mobile radio frequency radiation with the levels of piping distress by bees in their hive showed how RFR (radio frequency radiation) is contributing to the 70-80 fall in bee and insect populations over the last decade – *international journal of research 2020*

New review showing RFR harm on insects
Of 83 studies 72 found an effect. Negative effects include disturbed orientation. Reduced fertility, lethargy, changes in flight dynamics, failure to find food, reduced reaction speeds, escape behaviour, disturbance of the circadian rhythm, blocking of the respiratory chain and damage to the mitochondria, miss-activation of the immune system, and increased number of DNA strand breaks. EMFs effect the metabolism affecting voltage-gated calcium channels in neuro-transmission and in muscle tissue, leading to oxidative cell stress
The results show that EMF could seriously impact the vitality of insect populations and harmful effect occurred after several months. Field strengths 100 times below the ICNIRP limits* could already have effects. Insect habitats should be protected from existing high intensity EMF exposure.
How mobile phone radiation may be killing insects (18th Sept 2020).
Johanne Enssle, head of Germany's Nature and Biodiversity Conservation Union (NABU), said 'The subject is uncomfortable for many of us because it interferes with our daily habits and there are powerful economic interests behind mobile communication technology.'
　　　　*Industry dominated standards

5G RFR causes insect extinction?
On November 19th 2019 a 5G antenna was placed 250m from Angela's house in Melbourne, Australia 'The next day we saw bees dropping on the driveway then dying.' Two months later their garden is silent and barren. 'We have no insects - none. Our cumquat once laden all year has no new fruit coming. No olives on the way on our olive tree so laden last year. We dug soil yesterday - no worms either – nothing - all gone'.
Arthur Firstenberg January 30th 2020.
Arthur Firstenberg is currently running an online campaign to protect the bees from 5G in New Zealand

Meanwhile at the top of the chain – The US government has released a scientific report (Dec 5 2020) stating that *'Directly pulsed RF energy appears to be the most plausible mechanism'* for the illness suffered by US and Canadian diplomats in Cuba and China.

Brain damage to the diplomats and families from these microwave weapons as shown in MR scans, along with the other symptoms, such as fatigue, headaches and memory loss fit with the symptom of non-thermal Electromagnetic Hypersensitivity established in the literature since the 1930's.

Mobile phones and Wifi also use pulsed microwaves. The RF radiation injuries were judged clearly not psychological.

US pilot: surge in cancer and mental effects causing crashes

'Some US fighter pilots believe that radiation from the powerful radars on their aircraft have contributed to a surge in cancer cases among their ranks…the Pentagon is admitting a disturbing possibility that cockpit radiation may be affecting the mental judgement of pilots so badly that it is causing them to crash their aircraft.' *Microwave News Sept 16 2020*

The air is now carrying electrosmog of 1,000,000,000,000,000,000 more microwaves than 30 years ago.

"Eat Dirt and Thrive"

The above is a quote from the heading of a lecture by one of America's best qualified and most experienced and respected medical practitioners, Dr Zach Bush. It can be seen along with his growing number of presentations on the internet. Before continuing, I must define the true meaning of 'dirt' that I met up with when exploring the possibilities of gardening up here after we arrived in 1975. The American centre for healthy living, The Rodale Institute, in following their simple principle, 'healthy soil = healthy plants = healthy people defined 'dirt' as following –

One of the most unfortunate accidents of language in modern times is the equating of soil and dirt with the notion of defilement. The soil is not dirty, it is not unclean, it is not of itself productive of disease, it produces life. It is life. The soil is as alive as the teeming center of a city – more so. 'The gardener's guide to better soil 1975'. Modern science, Zach points out was disappointed to discover that human genes could only be counted as 20,000, midway between a flea, 30,000 and fruit fly 13,000. As a young medical student he was told that as practitioners his was the first generation to be able to identify future health vulnerabilities and the appropriate medications from a patient's genes. He points out to his audience that within the last ten years we as humans are assessed to have the support of 50 trillion cells each carrying one metre of DNA and in length would wrap 2 million times around the earth. We are dependent on our relationships with the natural world, and in particular the soil which we are destroying at an alarming rate with the constant downpour of glyphosate (Roundup) on our soils, in our food and impacting on the 'city of life' within our bodies described as the microbiome.

As a self-confessed 'dirty old man' I commend this and his other presentations to members.
Raymond

The Special Relationship

It must be no surprise that revelations arising from the identification and study of the microbiomes of humans, plants and the soil should lead to a rediscovery of the works of Sir Albert Howard and Lady Eve Balfour. In 'The Living Soil' 1943, Lady Balfour from her own researches and the testimony of farmers, was so convinced of an important link between these three in passing health up the line that she was active in calling for the amalgamation of the then Ministry of Health and the Ministry of Agriculture, with a soil specialist to be present in every hospital. She felt at the time more evidence from scientific studies would prove conclusive. Since then more than 30,000 scientific papers have been published on the subject of the bionutrients so far discovered in plants since 2000. The soil itself has been compared to a modern city, by one writer. Fungal links taken up by the plant have been described as *The World Wide Web* adding a mining and delivery service to its communication business. Other microbes swarm around the roots of plants providing security from the marauding hordes that would destroy the plant. While battles rage below ground, other microbes rise with the plant coating leaves and stems. Meanwhile this large workforce of 'city workers' needs to be fed. The plants own bacteria *the chloroplasts* are busy making use of sunlight, water and the mineral deliveries below ground to provide the magic (of muck and magic ?) to produce a great variety of what we refer to as phytochemicals in order to feed its workers. Over 8000 of these have been identified to date and each plant is said to produce several hundred of them. It is claimed that many more of these are yet to be discovered. Because plants are unable to move, the specialist services for which the chemicals are produced include protection from insects, disease, damaging ultraviolet light, inclement weather and browsing animals - *and ourselves.*

It is clear that the plants aren't fashioned to feed humans but over the years we have evolved alongside plants depending on them for nutrition and protection from disease. One particular group of chemicals that is present in plants known as antioxidants is said to provide us with protection from noxious particles known as *free radicals* that can inflame our artery linings, turn our normal cells cancerous, damage our eyesight, increase our risk of becoming obese and diabetic, and intensify the visible signs of aging. Among the growing number of benefits identified in eating plants and supported in small case studies have been an improvement in athletic performance, a lowering of the risk of infection, an increased ability to fight the 'flu, the lowering of blood pressure, lowering of LDL cholesterol, speeding up weight loss, protection for the aging brain, improved mood and boosted immunity. At the top of the chain is the newly born child and the richness of its growing microbiome introduced by its mother, will depend greatly on how well it will be able to form its own special relationship with a fertile soil.

Raymond.

And Finally The Quick Summary Of Healing Index; Most wild plants are good for everything but here are specific issues that spring to mind that some plants are **great** for!

Anti-cancer plants; Alexanders, Burdock, Cleavers, Herb Robert Grass, Sea Beet, Sea Buckthorn, Self Heal and Yarrow.

Antibiotic effects; Mullein (also use Nasturtium and Oregano; not in this book.)

Anti-parasitic; Mullein, Pineapple Weed, Sorrel (also research Wormwood.)

Arthitus/Joints; Black Mustard, Cleavers, Pennywort, Yarrow, Thistle

Bandage; Dock leaf

Blood Cleanse; Cleavers Grass

Breathing, Coughs and clearing mucus; *Cleaver, Clover, Cowslip, Eyebright, Mallow, Mallow, Mullein, Nettle, Pneapple Weed.* (Also use onions directly on the ribs see Bruton-Seal's, 'Kitchen Medicine or blend raw Garlic, Cayenne Pepper, Oregano oil, local honey and lemon together and take daily x4 times daily.)

Chronic Fatigue; *Dandelions*, Nettle, Seaweed, Yarrow

Depression; *Cowslip*, *Gorse, Nettle, Yarrow, Pennywot, Rock Samphire.*

Digestion; *Alexander, Dandelion Hogweed, Plantain, Three Cornered leek, Rosebay Willow Herb.*

Detox with; *Cleavers, Dandelion, Sorrel*

Diabetes; *Cleavers, Herb Robert, Nettles, Pennywort, Sorrel.*

Earache; *Mullein*

Eyes issues; *Eyebright, Dandelion.*

Fever; *Clover, Pineappleweed, Sorrel, Yarrow.*

Heart; *Hawthorn, Yarrow (also research Cayenne Pepper.)*

Immunity; *Cleavers, Dandelion, Herb Robert, Nettles, Sea Buckthorn, Self Heal.*

Liver; *Burdock, Cleavers, Dandelions, Sea Beet, Sorrel, Sowthistle, Thistle.*

Menstruation; *Alexander, Hogweed, Lady's Mantle, Yarrow.*

Menopause; *Red Clover, Dandelion, Lady's Mantle.*

Nettles stings and bites; *Plantain, Yarrow.*

Rejuvenating/making whole again; *Cleavers, Dandelions, Dock Grass, Herb Robert, Hogweed, Nettles, Pennywort, Rock Samphire, Rosebay Willow Herb, Sea Holly, Seaweed, Sow Thistle, Thistle.*

Skin; *Clover, Dandelion, Self Heal, Sea Buckthorn, Pennywort.*

Toothache; *Herb Bennet, Mallow*

Thyroid issues; *Cleavers, Hawthorn, Seaweed.*

Ulcers; *Alexanders, Hogweed, Mallow, Plantain.*

Further Reading And Resources Books

1. 'Health From God's Garden' (Austrian some great recipes and uses.) Maria Treben.

2. Edible And Medicinal Wild Plants Of Britain And Ireland by Robin Harford.

3. Food For Free by Richard Mabey.

4. Foraging in Spring by Robin Harford.

5. Foraging in summer by Robin Harford.

6. Hedgerow Medicine by Julie Bruton Seale.

7. Julia Levy (nomadic gypsy from wealthy jewish family)..DVD and herb books.

8. Knowledge To Forage by Dane de Luca Mulandiee.

9. Maurice Messegue..Health Secrets Of Plants And Herbs.

10. Plants For The People.. Erin Lovell Verinder.

11. The Holistic Herbalist by David Hoffmann; times to gather and uses.

12. The Wild Wisdom Of Weeds by Katrina Blair.

13. 'Why Suffer? By Ann Wigmore. (see GRASS and inspirationalpeople at the end .)

14. The Ultimate Dandelion Medicine Book by Kristina Seleshanko.

15. Witch's Garden by Sandra Lawrence.

16. Seaweeds of Britain and Ireland by Francis Bunker

17. The Seaweed revolution by Vincent Doumeizel (see page)

Closer to home/Local books

1. 'Seaweed Foraging In Cornwall And The Isles Of Scilly.' By Rachel Lambert.

2. 'Wild Food Foraging In Cornwall And The Isles Of Scilly.' By Rachel Lambert.

3. Never Mind The Burdock by Emma Gunn.

4. River Cottage Edible Sea Shore by John Wright.

5. The Sensory Herbal Handbook by The Seed Sistas.

6. Plants For A Future by Ken Fern.

Additional

1. Acetaria; A Disourse in Sallets by John Evelyn

2. 'Our Stolen future' (Breasts cancer cells, pollution in The womb, EDCs.) by Theo Coleburn.

3. Common Herbs For Natural Health; Juliette de Bairacli Levy (Julia Of The Herbs.).

4. Elixirs Of Life by Mrs C.F Leyel (1948)

5. Fertility From The Ocean Deep (The fertile Mile) Charles Walters.

6. Hawthorn by Bill Vaughn.

7. Herbs For Daily Use by Mary Thorne Quelch (1941.)

8. In Search Of The Mother Trees by Suzanne Humphries.

9. Sea Around Us by Rachel Carson.

10. Sea Energy Agriculture..' by Maynard Murray.

11. The Hundred Year Lie by Raymond Fitzgerald.

12. Untangled Life by Mervyn Sheldrake.

Other Ppl to follow on film and YouTube

1. 'Fantastic Fungi' film and books by Paul Stammets.

2. Babara O'Neil..'The origin Of all Disease' plus other videos.

3. Galoway Wild Food..fab website and a great friendly organisation.

4. Julia's Wild Weeds; Natural remedies part 1 and 2

5. Six Inches Of Soil. Regenerative farming SET IN CORNWALL

6. The Invisible Rainbow by Arthur Firstenburg

7. You Tube; Raymond's Wisdom. Watch some of Ray's teachings and me.

8. Zach Bush (Roundup/ Glysophates, Spiritual, ecological steps to move forwards) You Tube

Useful Terms

- **Analgesic**; Relieves pain.

- **Anti coagulant**...Inhibits blood coagulation.

- **Anti oxidant;** Have uneven electrons but only want to steal from free radicals..so they are molecules that fight free radicals e.g E and C vitamins and Flavanoids (mineral) unstable highly reactive molecules are antioxidants.

- **Astringent:** Causes tissues and mucous membranes to contract.

- **Cholagogue**; Increases bile production

- **Cartenoids;** Phytonutrients that are plant pigments responsible for bright orange and yellow hues help photosynthesis in plants and act as an antioxidant for free radicals. Converted by the body to Vitamin A and have an Anti Inflammatory, and immunity booster action on the body. Need fat to be absorbed.

- **Decoction**, concentrated liquid from heating or boiling a plant.

- **EDCs**: Endocrine Disruptive Chemicals (Coleburn.)

- **Emollient**: Protects, softens and soothes the skin.

- **Enzymes**; Proteins that are biological catalyst that help digest food, fight toxins, produce energy although the body has a set amount of enzymes, they can be found in certain raw foods as heat kills them. Pineapple, Mango, Advocado to name just a few and without a doubt some foraged plants will contain enzymes. Without these sometimes consumed nutrients will not be carried from cell to cell..hence the importance of eating raw and wild food.

- **Expectorant..**Encourages phlegm and mucus to shift from the throat and lungs.

- **Flavonoids;** comes from the latin 'yellow' (*Flavus*) responsible for colours in plants that attracts the bees and ward off predators, they have anti inflammatory qualities, can protect the skin are anti inflammatory, anti cancer and can boost the immune system. Mainly in fruit and vegetables.

- **Free Radicals** Compounds that can cause harm if their levels become too high but are useful for fighting infection for example in the right amounts, uneven number of electrons so they need to take an electron which is great for certain situations like infection but long term they can take from healthy cells causing damage

- **Germanium;**High in some plants such as Aloe Vera, Ginger, Shitake Mushrooms, Comfrey, onions, garlic some fungi and Herb Robert, lowers Oxygen requirement in the body and increases Oxygen levels; so helps fight free radicals and cancer. Carries electrical signals from cell to cell in plants and the human body.

- **Minerals** Inorganic nutrients e.g Potasium, Calcium, Selenium, Chromium, Zinc, Copper needed in macro or micro form for the body to function well.(*)

- **Mycellium;** Physical body of the fungus above ground.

- **Mycorrhizae** *Literally translates to "fungus-root." Mycorrhiza defines a (generally) mutually beneficial relationship between the root of a plant and* *a fungus that colonizes the plant root. In many plants, Mycorrhiza are fungi that grow inside the plant's roots, or on the surfaces of the roots. The plant and the fungus have a mutually beneficial relationship, where the fungus facilitates water and nutrient uptake in the plant, and the plant provides food and nutrients created by photosynthesis to the fungus. This exchange is a significant factor in nutrient cycles and the ecology, evolution, and physiology of plants.' (biologydictionary.net.)*

- **Nervine** relaxes and calms the nervous system.

- **Neuroregenerative** Promotes and regenerates the nervous system.

- **Phytonutrients** Plant based compounds that have beneficial effects on the body include Flavanoids, carotenoids..can have antioxidant and antiflammatory qualities.

- **Polyphenols** Polyphenols are plant compounds with antioxidant and anti-inflammatory properties that may lower blood sugar, blood pressure, and heart disease risk

- **Polysaccharides;** Long chain sugars including starch and Glycogen, Cellulose and Inulin. Whilst glycogen and C starch provide short term energy stores, cellulose builds cell wall structure and inulin has hypoglycaemic properties and is good for regulating blood.

- **Purgative**..Causes the evacuation of the bowls.

- **Saponins:** Derived from soapwort plant as they taste soapy and create saliva. Used to protect the plant from Microbes and Fungi and although poisonous to fish, humans can tolerate them and they often produce a expectorant quality as they irritate mucous membrane in the gut.

- **Vitamins;** Fat or water soluble organic nutrients; phytonutrients, antioxidants and some enzymes e.g Vitamin C, K, A and Folic Acid.(*)

- **Wort;** Of worth and usually valued medicinally.

- (*Both vitamins and minerals are vital to release energy from food and vital for cell reaction and boosting immunity....so will contain enzymes and antioxidants etc for this role.)

Latin plant names and stories behind them.

Started by Carl Linnaeus in 18th century for a universal recognition as plants have so many names across the world.

Genus and species or Family/ group and characteristics, leaf shape colour etc . Particularly in foraging these can indicate its healing or medicinal qualities.

Genus and species =binomial.. *in italics.*

e.g **argentea**; silver. **maculate**; spotted, **angustifolia**; narrow leaves, **nana** ;small/compact, **japonica**;Japan, **amoenus**;attractive , **vulgaris**;common.

Taraxacum refers to 'manydisorders' so Dandelions can treat many disorders

Officinalis ..belonging to official..store room of a monastery where medicines are kept so used medicinally.

Wort.. from wyrt and will often indicate meaning plant, root or herb and considered beneficial so really of worth but if prefixed by an organ it often indicates they looked like a part of the human so must be good for them..i.e Lungwort, Bladderwort, Liverwort.

Artemisia varieties in plant names; Roman goddess Diana was the huntress and in Greek her name was Artemis the moon goddess and many plants with the name Artemisia cast a silvery moon on leaves. Artemesia was also the protector of small children and helped her Mother deliver her twin brother Apollo after she had been born.So it stands to reason that Artemisia plant species such as **Mugwort** are used in labour to help birth the baby. Mugwort stimulates Oxytocin the hormone released during birth.

Achilles (see Yarrow) Achilles used Yarrow 'Archilles Millefolium' in battle on his soldiers to stop bleeding.

A summary of Some Of Vincent Doumeizels' Seaweed Revolution and how Seaweed could save our Planet.

Seaweed; A Plants that could save the planet?
Seaweed is a Macroalgae ;one of the first plants on the planet after Microalgae Seaweed even by its name is undervalued. In parts of Asia it is referred to as **Sea Vegetables** or **Sea Forests** and a great book to get your head around the potential of this amazing nutritional food it is a good idea to read Vincent Douemeizel's book The Seaweed Revolution in which he portrays the incredible potential of seaweed not just as a food but to save the world; and here are some really important points;
Environmentally; The sea or Seaweed provides 50% of the oxygen we need on earth it also is one of the most efficient species to capture Carbon and no greater example of this are the Kelp Forests in Penzance Bay. The biomass of Seaweed is greater than the mass of all forests on the Earth and it captures 3 times more Carbon per Hectare than the Amazon Forest. **Think of the sea forests as our second lung!**
Seaweed does not need water or chemicals to grow its nutrition is from the sea so it does need roots but has a stipe to hold it to the rocks.
If we could harvest and eat more Seaweed naturally it could allow us to rest and replenish the soils which are now dead from being sprayed and over fertilized. Seaweed could also replace plastic, cotton and be used as fertiliser. Seaweed slows waves down so helps prevent coastal erosion. It also grows at great speeds of a few metres over days, it can replace itself quickly.
In fact if Seaweed was used naturally in Cattle feed and Fish farms it would prevent disease and stop the overuse of antibiotics in sea and land mammals.
Seaweed does not need packaging and can be easily transported once dried.

Over 100s of years Sheep in a Scottish Island known as Ronaldsay have adapted their diet to eat just Seaweed, the results being their meat and wool is famous for its quality and not only that but **they reduce Methane emissions by 80%!!**

Water extracted from Seaweed does not contain salt so could be useful for water shortages.

With all that in mind and although we use Seaweed in many foods, particularly red seaweed which is known for its Alganite content which thickens food, we do not use this valuable ancient algae enough we utilise and farm about 2million square Kilometres (mainly in Asia) when in fact there are over 48 million square Kilometres of Seaweed and it is fast growing so extraction could be sustainable.

Nutritionally, Seaweed is a low fat high protein food source full of long chain Omega 3s; DHA and EPAs. It contains high Vitamin Contents, it is loaded with Vitamin B, Magnesium,Phosphorous, Zinc and Iodine. The high Iodine levels can be a saving grace for the Thyroid but it can also be detrimental for the condition. Unfortunately this is the reason it has been dismissed as a food source by Europe, when in fact the cut off criteria is much higher in Asia and Japan where they thrive on Seaweed. Cooking Seaweed reduces its Iodine content by 90% which could rectify this concern.

Iodine is a volatile chemical so often displaces itself from salt and in Mountainous areas gets washed away; areas creating Thyroid and goitre issues. Iodine deficiency can cause fatigue, constipation, depression , and weight gain. It is estimated. In Africa for example that 86 million people are goitre sufferers. Iodized salt or seaweed consumption could solve this and malnutrition problems.

Interesting Facts; Our development may have been helped by Seaweed after skeletons were discovered in a cave in South America after a farmer diverted a river in the 1970s. The remains were said to be about 14 to 18 thousand years old and they had travelled from Asia along the 'Kelp Highway' within the cave 23 different types of dried Seaweed were discovered meaning this was one of their main food sources.

The Vikings used to carry dried Seaweed they were wise because when the devastating disease of Scurvy was recognised it was treated with oranges and lemons, the link with Vitamin C had not been established, however the high levels of Vitamin C in seaweed meant the cure to this awful deathly disease was right underneath the suffering sailors!

Green Seaweed is closely linked to Grass, Strawberries and Oak Trees,than the Red and Brown varieties it grows next to. They are all worlds away in plant family links. However cleverly they are known to communicate through electrical impulses to send warnings to each other of danger or to attract the predator of whatever is attacking them!

I hope you have enjoyed this book and are looking forward to making nature a bigger part of your life and as Ray said 'Count Your Blossoms not your Blessings.'

Above centre Ray with his wife Sylvia right pouring the flask with a local gardening group.

"The shore is an ancient world, for as long as there has been an earth and sea there has been this place of the meeting of land and water. Yet it is a world that keeps alive the sense of continuing creation and of the relentless drive of life. Each time that I enter it, I gain some new awareness of its beauty and its deeper meanings, sensing that intricate fabric of life by which one creature is linked with another, and each with its surroundings." Rachel Carson (The Edge Of The Sea.)

The Hawthorn; A portal for Fairies and magic; Do not chop a Hawthorn down unless you want to upset the magical people! Now go enjoy the hedgerow!

Printed in Great Britain
by Amazon